Mere Creatures of the State?

Mere Creatures of the State?
Education, Religion, and the Courts
A View from the Courtroom

William Bentley Ball

CRISIS BOOKS
A Publication of the Orestes Brownson Society
Notre Dame, Indiana
1994

To my wife, Caroline

Contents

Foreword

TO SAY THAT SOMEONE IS A CHAMPION in the way that I say William Bentley Ball is a champion is to say something about one's view of history. It is to draw one's sword against every form of determinism, to defy the dismal doctrine that reduces human beings to ciphers in the great roaring machine of putatively inevitable change. History is not a machine, nor is it a process driven by impersonal forces, countervailing interests, technological imperatives, or the logic of progress. History is people. To be sure, forces, interests, and imperatives beyond numbering enter into it, and importantly so. But history is, most importantly, people who Oppose the wrong and contend for the right. That is to say, people like William Bentley Ball.

Given the formidable force of the wrong opposed by this book, and given what may appear to be the improbability of achieving the right for which Bill Ball contends, some may think his effort just a bit Quixotic. But that would be a serious mistake. He is not jousting against windmills but against patterns of thought and practice that have achieved an awesome dominance in American life and law. Moreover, his life's work was demonstrated again and again the power of the individual to effectively challenge that dominance. From the Supreme Court to school board hearings in humble villages, the voice of Bill Ball has championed the cause of "little people" who have dared to question the authority of their supposed betters. His advocacy joins fortitude to compassion, learning to eloquence, and earnestness to humor. It is a mix of virtues too rarely encountered.

Religious freedom is his passion. Some, intending no compliment, might say it his obsession. Would to God we were all so obsessed. Bill Ball understands, as too few do understand, that religious freedom is the first freedom; it is the source and shield of every other human freedom. It is the first freedom in the Constitution, being the first clause of the First Amendment. But that is not what makes it the first freedom. What makes it the first freedom is that religion marks the capacity of the human person to enter into communion with the Absolute, with God. By that relationship with God, all other relationships are relativized and transformed. Today this truth must be asserted most urgently against the ambitions of the modern state, and especially against the pretension of the state to claim ownership of our children.

But let me step back just a little, lest that sound too apocalyptic. When in America, a reader might ask, has the state ever claimed to own our children? In Nazi Germany and Soviet Russia, certainly. In some other countries, maybe. But in the United States of America? It is true that one can search through all the law books of the land and not come up with any instance in which the federal or state governments have flatly said that the state owns the children of the society. But there is nothing at all apocalyptic about pointing out, as this book does, that the state has frequently acted as though it owns the children. And, in some of the court decisions examined here, the state has made that claim at least obliquely and by implication. The concerns raised by Bill Ball are alarming, to be sure, but they are not alarmist.

The modern state views religion as an anomaly; it is at least a nuisance and at worst a threat. This is not surprising. After all, religion posits another sovereignty, a superior sovereignty, against the sovereignty of the state. The modern state understands itself to have a monopoly on sovereignty. It understands itself to be the supreme authority. Religion, when religion has the courage to be authentic, says No. It says No because it has said Yes to a higher sovereignty, the sovereignty of God. To the mind of the modern secularist, this is intolerable. It is disruptive, it is divisive, it is sectarian, it is parochial, it is, in a word, intolerable. As Bill Ball convincingly demonstrates, the mind of the modern secularist has increasingly become the mind of our courts.

It was not always this way in America. The genuinely new thing, the audaciously radical thing, about the American experiment is that the founders specifically designed a government that would be accountable to higher sovereignties. First, the sovereignty of the people of course—an idea that is foundational to democratic theory and practice. Then, and most important, the sovereignty of whatever sovereignty is acknowledged by the people. As, for instance, in "one nation under God." That much-later addition to the Pledge of Allegiance means a nation under judgment, a nation accountable to a higher sovereignty, to the Supreme Sovereign. The Religion Clause of the First Amendment anticipated and constitutionally secured that understanding of limited government. But a lot has happened in the past two centuries, and especially in the last half century.

In court decisions since World War II, and notably in decisions having to do with religion and education, the state has asserted an ever-more-expansive claim over the society. Religion, which originally had a privileged place in the constitutional scheme of things, is increasingly penalized by state policy. When religion is penalized, it follows that the institutions of religion are penalized. This means, above all, the churches and the family. The churches and the family inculcate devotion to and publicly assert allegiance to the higher sovereignty. The state can only realize its ambition of unlimited authority by limiting the authority of rival institutions.

The Religion Clause contains a "no establishment" provision and a "free exercise" provision. The purpose or the end of the Clause is the free exercise of religion. No establishment is a means to that end. The reason for no establishment is that, if one religion were established, it would violate the free exercise of religion by those who do not belong to the established religion. It all makes perfect sense. The curious thing that has happened, however, is that the means (no establishment) has now been turned into the end, and the end (free exercise) is viewed as a terrible nuisance. No establishment is now taken to mean that any cooperative relationship between government and religion is suspect as a forbidden establishment of religion. Government space must be "religion free." And since government space is increasingly thought to be the same thing as public space, the result is that all public space must be "religion free." Wherever the government goes, religion must retreat, and today the government goes almost everywhere.

But please do not get the wrong idea. This is not a book about constitutional theory or legal philosophy. Well, it is that too. But it is mainly a book about people, about how they strive to order their lives by their deepest convictions, about how they work to transmit to their children the best that they are and believe, and about how government in this country has too often become the enemy of their finest aspirations. It is also a book about what can be done to renew this American experiment in freedom that is ordered to the virtue and truth of biblical religion. Finally, and although he will be embarrassed by my saying it, this is a book that demonstrates the courage and wisdom of a champion who will not give up. He is the kind of person who, by the grace of God, makes history.

Richard John Neuhaus
SS. Peter and Paul, 1994
New York City

Acknowledgments

I AM GRATEFUL TO A VALUED FRIEND and Presbyterian minister, Rev. Keith Crim, for having urged me, years ago, to write of cases in which I have been involved—more recently, and especially, to Dr. Ralph McInerny, publisher of *Crisis*, who suggested this Crisis Book. I am indebted to Monsignor George A. Kelly, founder of the Fellowship of Catholic Scholars, Father Richard John Neuhaus, Judge John T. Noonan, Jr., and Dr. John A. Hostetler, for their encouragement. Two treasured friends, Edward B. Hanify, Esq., of Boston, and Dr. Howard J. Fetterhoff, of Harrisburg, offered me valuable comment on the manuscript. To my wife, Caroline, and my daughter, Virginia Duncan, I owe thanks for their constant support in this project. Without the skill and patience of Dianne Haverl, my secretary for thirty-four years, this book would not have appeared. I thank my brother and sister lawyers of Ball, Skelly, Murren & Connell who have shared many of the adventures with me to which this book refers. As I write, I am mourning the loss of another who shared them, as an expert on the witness stand in three major cases, that noble scholar, Christian, and friend, Russell Amos Kirk.

Religion in the Dock

Introduction: Why This Book?

"IT IS NOT FAIR!"

My diary shows that I sounded that as a rallying cry for the Rob Roy Clan in its great struggle against the oppressor, Bud Utter. We did prevail—the battlefield, I clearly recall, looking like the battle-field of Aghrim described by Macauley—"white with the bones of the vanquished." Probably you have never heard of our triumph that day. The media treated it with calculated silence. Further, it happened on October 6, 1923, when most of you weren't born. Yes, I have that date right. It was my seventh birthday, and the tyrant Utter was then nine—a big fellow who made life miserable for us of the second grade at William McKinley Elementary. But we of the Rob Roy Clan routed him and his henchmen on that Sloan Avenue vacant lot!

On October 6, seven decades later, I found myself delivering much the same message about "fairness" to judges of a United States Court of Appeals—this time in defense of a victim of outrageous religious stereotyping by government officials. So the compulsions of my childhood seem to have stuck with me. The road between then and now has taken me many places protesting that one thing or another was "not fair"—in particular, to the courts of law of twenty-two states and, on ten occasions, to the Supreme Court of the United States. No, I am not one of those luminaries of the legal world whom the media acclaim as "champions of unpopular causes." By and large, the cases I have tried have been *un*popular "unpopular causes," causes rarely favored by our liberal media. Nor have my clients been the rich and famous. Mostly, they have been nobodies, at least in this world's eyes.

Some of these causes—two cases in particular—will be the subject of this book. I beg you not to be put off by the fact that this is a book about law, written by a lawyer. I will not be talking with you in lawyerese (e.g., "the named insured, except as provided in Section 3(a), shall be entitled to the marginal amounts set forth in Section 10(g),") or even in lawprofessorese (e.g., "partially over-ruling *Pugg v. Gashouse*, the Court, in a plurality opinion by Justice Blackmun relied upon progeny of *Queasy*, such as *Thor v. Toop*. But see the Brennan concurrence in the latter."). This lawyer's task in communicating is made very easy by the fact that the cases I discuss are dramas, stories of real people and remarkable events. No, they are not dramas involving the fingerprints on the gun, the telltale lingerie, or Exhibit A, the blood-stained glove. They involve matters of far greater dramatic significance (when you come to think about it): religious freedom, rights of conscience, and the great question overarching our times: How far the state shall have power over our lives.

Published writing on these matters is mostly scholarly comment on appellate court opinions—much of it extremely valuable. Yet this commentary often provides but a part of the picture of cases under discussion. It will often be confined to observing and evalu-ating the conflicting points of view of judges and tell little or nothing of the real actors involved. The *whole* picture of a case, however, will disclose not only principles but people—how they came to be in court, what was at stake in their lives, or how a particular law involving them was generated by the competition of ideas and groups in the turmoil of lobbies and legislatures. This "view from below," I feel, is helpful to a better understanding of the "view from above" (courts' opinions). Hence this book and its main focus on the former.

Of Bleak Houses, Lagado, and the Court That Is Supreme

THE COMMON IMPRESSION APPEARS to be that peoples' rights are determined in lawsuits. But sometimes they are not. A case, at best, goes through a series of stages, like a product which begins with raw materials, then is processed through a succession of steps, and finally is finished. A litigant rightly hopes that his case will at least progress from the "raw material" stage to an ultimate judgment which is arguably rational. But what is generated from counsel table and bench—the presentation of evidence, the examining of witnesses, the counterpoint of judges' questions and rulings, and, often, the outbreak of the unexpected—may dash that hope. Cases are sometimes baseless affairs which ought never to have been brought or which are botched by the attorney or which are thrown out by judges due either to the baselessness, the attorney's botching, or His Honor's own botching. Some cases are skewed by bright clerks of malleable judges. Finally there is the case which enters a maze, travels about in that maze, and, somewhere in it, simply dies. Such was the fate of the case of poor Shelton College, crawling about in the judicial maze, in eight courts for six years—until at last, half won and half lost, by a nine-word order of the Supreme Court, it expired.[1] Here was a sorry instance of "the wearying down of the right" which Dickens described in *Bleak House*. In ever so many cases courts do *not* determine rights.

I well realize that we in this country are drowning in law (which may be why we have so many lawyers) or drowning in lawyers (which may be why we have so many laws). Law in its procedural aspects is sometimes exquisitely complicated. It must also be true that some of our judges were graduated from the legal equivalent of Swift's Grand Academy of Lagado, and we can only wish that they might devote their marvelously complicated minds to experimenting with dogs rather than with people. Leaving them aside, the very nature of legal processes often calls for what the layman may regard as hair-splitting but which may in fact be a necessary distinguishing or defining of things.

Largely uncritically, Americans accept the idea that their Supreme Court, in many instances, has final say in their public affairs. They have witnessed vast social changes, affecting their lives in the most intimate way, brought about by a vote taken, not by the elected representatives of 240 million Americans, but among nine citizens who are not elected—indeed the single vote of one among the nine sometimes deciding a question of stupendous national importance. In the media we often hear a litigant's lawyer forthrightly declare: "I'll take this case to the Supreme Court!" Take it there he may, but the chances of its staying there are utterly remote. More than 5,000 cases are filed with the Supreme Court each term. Many are filed, but few are chosen. Plenary review by the Court through the submitting of briefs and oral argument is granted in but a tiny fraction (for the 1993 Term, 3 percent) of the cases filed. In most litigations, therefore, the appealed decision of a lower court is left standing.

Less than a dozen cases involving religion were decided by the Supreme Court in the first century and a half following 1789. Only in the 1940s, after the Court had held that the Religion Clauses of the First Amendment apply to the states,[2] did a gradually increasing

---

1   *New Jersey-Philadelphia Presbytery of the Bible Presbyterian Church v. New Jersey State Board of Education*, 469 U.S. 1107 (1985).

2   The clauses read: "Congress shall make no law respecting an establishment of religion or prohibiting the free exercise thereof." As adopted, that clause restricted only the federal government ("Congress"). The

flow of decisions in religious cases issue from the Supreme Court. In the 1993 Term, thirty-six cases involving religion were brought to the Court.

Yet it is to the Supreme Court that people whose religious liberties are troubled by government turn for guidance—not indeed for guidance of the conscience but only to ascertain what protections the Court has said that the Constitution allows to manifestations of conscience. The guide is not infallible and frequently lacks consistency. Up to the middle of the 19th Century, the Court could be said to have a philosophy—a philosophy reflecting the Protestant Christian ethos. Even as late as 1892, the Court, in a unanimous opinion, felt comfortable in stating that "this is a Christian nation." [3] The Court, in a lengthy affirmation of the theistic religious character of the nation, said:

> If we examine the constitutions of the various states we find in them a constant recognition of religious obligation. Every constitution of every one of the forty-four states contains language which either directly or by clear implication recognizes a profound reverence for religion and an assumption that its influence in all human affairs is essential to the well being of the community.

That statement would scarcely be made by the justices today; indeed they proceed from no common philosophical base. It is for that reason that I am little excited by commentary on the Court typically given in the media today—that is, that the Court is split between "liberals" and "conservatives," or that one or another justice, the sensible middle-of-the-roader, is a "swing vote" between the two.. Not true, because the justices know no road. Our Supreme Court justices less and less operate out of the great patrimony of law rooted in the ancient traditions out of which the

---

Fourteenth Amendment, in 1868, barred states from depriving any person of life, liberty or property without due process of law. In recent times the Supreme Court has held the Establishment and Free Exercise Clauses of the First Amendment to apply to the states through the "due process" clause of the Fourteenth Amendment.

3   *Church of the Holy Trinity v. United States*, 143 U.S. 457, 471 (1892).

Constitution sprang, and more and more render decisions *ad hoc* on the basis of secular utility. But the story of our jurisprudence for the third century of the Bill of Rights remains to be told.

"Rights of Peculiar Delicacy"

"[R]ights of conscience are, in their nature, of peculiar delicacy, and will little bear the gentlest touch of the governmental hand." So spoke Daniel Carroll, of Maryland, on August 15, 1789, in urging the House of Representatives to adopt an amendment to the American Constitution protecting religious freedom. While much of the ensuing debate over the amendment centered upon the dangers of establishing a state church, Carroll's point went deeper and reached more broadly. He was concerned not only about the liberties of churches as opposed to a state monopoly of religion but about rights of individuals to live out, or exercise, religious beliefs where conscience would leave them without alternative. Carroll saw the "governmental hand" as inherently heavy and hence to be restrained where the peculiarly delicate thing of religious conscience might come in its way.

Carroll, not a supporter of ecclesiastical establishment, was also not a supporter of what some might deem its opposite: the Benthamite view that majorities may define liberties of religion. He was not unique in that respect. His co-contributors to the formulation of the Bill of Rights were of precisely the same conviction. None excepted from what had been said in the Declaration of Independence thirteen years earlier, that it is a "self- evident" truth that the "unalienable" rights of each of us are an endowment, not of any king, government, or majority (all of which are transitory) but of the unchanging God. The Declaration was, in a sense, the preamble to the Preamble to the Constitution, and the "rights" of which it spoke ("life, liberty, and the pursuit of happiness") were known to embrace freedom of religion.

There is good reason for calling religious liberty our First Freedom. Its protection is placed first, as the first of the ten amendments which make up the Bill of Rights, ahead of the protections of rights of speech, press, assembly, and petition. That placement does not indeed prove that religious liberty was deemed more important than the other First Amendment liberties, but one is entitled to doubt that the placement was accidental. All should agree that the freedom of religion prescribed in the Amendment's conjunction of liberties was not intended to be of lesser importance than the Amendment's other liberties.[4]

Further, there appeared a consensus that the First Amendment itself was deemed a sort of "survival amendment" in the Bill of Rights. Compare it, for example, with the Eighth Amendment, which forbids "cruel and unusual punishments." If today a law were passed providing that criminals be branded, the consensus undoubtedly is that that would be a "cruel and unusual punishment." But suppose that the courts held that it was not. Would that mean that there is no relief from such a statute? Not as long as the *First* Amendment exists because the First Amendment protects, for example, speech, press, assembly, and petition. We, the people, could use our speech, our press, and we could assemble and we could petition in order to get the legislature to repeal the branding statute. Those provisions protect the basic democratic processes, and it is plain to see why we can call those provisions "survival" provisions—provisions which, in a fundamental way, help us survive as a free people.

The protection of religious liberty was also plainly considered essential to national survival because religion itself was thought to be. The Northwest Ordinance, adopted by the Continental Congress in 1787, said that religion is necessary to good government and the happiness of mankind. Madison, in his Memorial and Remonstrance to the General Assembly of Virginia, had said that "[b]efore any man can be considered as a member of Civil Society, he must be considered as a subject of the Governour of the Universe." Jefferson, in his *Notes on Virginia*, asked: "Can the liberties of a nation be thought secure when we have removed their only firm

---

4   The development of the constitutions of the original states shows the same emphasis. See my article, "The Religion Clauses of the Pennsylvania Constitution," 3 *Widener Journal of Public Law*, 709 (1994).

basis, a conviction in the minds of the people that these liberties are a gift of God?"[5]

We are removed 200 years from the time those statements were made. Political leaders today still feel it useful to include an "under God" somewhere in a speech about the nation, but such curtsies may more illustrate the irrelevance of God than His immanence. Few would deny that a materialist spirit is rampant within American society, now radically altering its morals, its family life, its art, its entertainment, its education. This spirit tends to crowd religion, more and more displacing it. The result is a secular society—that is, one in which the role of theistic religion is greatly restricted in public life. As Richard John Neuhaus has stated:

> The idea is widely accepted that religion is something between an individual and his God. . . . Religion is the business of church and home and has no place in public space. These and other axioms are, it is commonly said, part of the American way. Legally and politically, they are supported by a notion of the "separation of church and state" that is understood to mean the separation of religion and religiously based morality from the public realm.[6]

A decline in the sense of the sacred is evident even in churches, once the abode solely of the sacred. But this secular society necessarily becomes a secularist society—that is, one whose *laws* come to express programs for solving society's insistent problems on the sole basis of material utility. These laws reinforce secularism.

This book might be entitled *Liberty at Twilight*. "Twilight," literally, means a state, partly light, partly dark, and that can signify what we find both at dawn and at the onset of night. Most readers will take it, I suppose, in the latter sense. I write out of no little concern that the latter sense may come to correspond to reality but in the hope that a heightened awareness of the vital significance of religious liberty may correct some emerging tendencies in the

---

5   As quoted by Canon Stokes. See A. P. Stokes, *Church and State in the United States*, vol. 1, 339.

6   R. J. Neuhaus, *The Naked Public Square*, 20.

newer jurisprudence of subjecting religion to the almost unlimited power of the secular state. As Christopher Dawson predicted sixty years ago,[7] the Materialist Society is marginalizing religion and expanding social programs which leave religion and its moral claims wholly out of account.

The American Constitution, in its First Amendment, had been wisely designed as a wall against unlimited state power affecting religion. Its Establishment Clause barred the setting up of a state church.[8] Its Free Exercise Clause forbade government to prohibit the observance of religion.

The Approach of Plato's Guardians

No area of the life of any nation is of greater importance to its future than that of education of the young. But it is precisely in that area of American life that Dawson's prediction has proved, over the past three-quarters of our century, alarmingly correct. A good beginning point from which to observe its fulfillment is Oregon in 1922. In that year, at a general election in the State of Oregon, an initiative was adopted making it a crime for parents to enroll their children in any but public schools. The state threatened to arrest and prosecute all parents who would send their children to private schools. The Act was inspired by the Imperial Council A. A. O. Nobles Mystic Shine, the Grand Lodge of Oregon, A. F. & A. M., and the Supreme Council, A. & A. S. Rite for the Southern Jurisdiction of

---

7   "The new state will be universal and omnicompetent. It will mould the mind and guide the life of its citizens from the cradle to the grave. It will not tolerate any interference with its educational functions by any sectarian organization, even though the latter is based on religious convictions. And this is the more serious, since the introduction of psychology into education has made the schoolmaster a spiritual guide as well as a trainer of the mind. In fact it seems as though the school of the future must increasingly usurp the functions that the Church exercised in the past, and that the teaching profession will take the place of the clergy as the spiritual power of the future." C. Dawson, *Religion and the Totalitarian State*, in R. Kirk, *The Conservative Reader*, 495.

8   See generally, R. T. Cord, *Separation of Church and State: Historical Fact and Current Fiction*.

the United States. The Nobles Mystic had circulated a pamphlet, supporting the public school monopoly, warning against people "forming groups," and saying that "[t]he permanency of this nation rests in the education of its youth in our public schools." "Our children," it said, "must not under any pretext, be it based upon money, creed or social status, be divided into antagonistic groups, there to absorb the narrow views of life, as they are taught." Befezzed and marching in oriental garb, these Americanist devotees of sacred signs and secret ceremonies nevertheless bade the voters: "Mix those with prejudices in the public school melting pot for a few years while their minds are plastic, and finally bring out the finished product, a true American." [9]

Three years later the Supreme Court would deal with a challenge to that statute. Meanwhile, in a Nebraska case upholding the freedom of a Lutheran school to teach German to children, the Court had reflected on the power of the state in reference to their "plastic" minds. It quoted Plato's "Ideal Commonwealth's" prescription that "children are to be common, and no parent is to know his own child nor any child his parent. . . . The proper officers will take the offspring . . . into the pen or fold." The Court noted that "[i]n order to submerge the individual and develop ideal citizens, Sparta assembled the males at seven into barracks and entrusted their subsequent education and training to official guardians. . ." [10] The Court vehemently rejected Plato's prescription. While the state may do much, it said, to improve the quality of its citizens, the desire of the legislature to "foster a homogeneous people with American ideals" would not justify the violation of fundamental rights.

Building upon that background, in 1925 the Court held Oregon's

---

9   *Oregon School Case—Complete Record*, 368–69. Professor Robert Ulich comes close to the same prescription when he suggests that teachers should "educate free minds, who, on the one hand, appreciate the depth of man's religious tradition, but to whom, on the other hand, *the old denominational and dualistic concepts appear secondary, if not inhibitive to, the formation of a unifying world outlook.*" Freund and Ulich, *Religion and the Public Schools*, 50. (Emphasis supplied.)

10   *Meyer v. Nebraska*, 262 U.S. 390, 401 (1923).

monopoly statute unconstitutional. The Society of Sisters of the Holy Names of Jesus and Mary, along with a secular military academy, had sued to bar imposition of the statute on private school parents. The Supreme Court, in its opinion, attacked the idea of a state educational monopoly, upheld the freedom of private (including religious) schools, and, in a memorable phrase, stressed parental rights in education: "*The child is not the mere creature of the state*; those who nurture him and direct his destiny have the right, coupled with the high duty, to recognize and prepare him for additional obligations." [11] In that context, the state would be permitted a narrow and limited regulatory role over schools in the name of the common good. But nothing in the *Pierce* decision suggested the state in the role of primary educator or, as superior educator, the standard setter for all educational endeavors. The holding in *Pierce* flatly contradicted blank-check public regulatory power over private education. *Pierce* was thus wholly consistent with the teachings of Catholics, Evangelicals, and Orthodox Jews on education and parental rights and in defense of religious schools and parental rights and duties. [12]

But in the decades following *Pierce*, the rights which it defined have come under attack. Precisely the situation envisioned by the Court, and scathingly rejected by it in *Pierce*, has come into existence, with enormous power claimed by the state over the education of the young. The public school system, massively supported by taxation, has achieved near monopoly. The public schools had reflected (albeit sometimes weakly) Protestant values, imparting traditional concepts of virtue. And the schools (with greater or lesser emphasis) had then acknowledged God through the employ-

---

11   *Pierce v. Society of Sisters of the Holy Names of Jesus and Mary*, 268 U.S. 510, 535 (1925). The Court held the Oregon program to violate that section of the Fourteenth Amendment which forbids any state to "deprive any person of life, liberty, or property without due process of law."

12   Declaration on Christian Education of Vatican Council II, *The Documents of Vatican II* (Abbott ed.), 644; National Association of Evangelicals, Convention Resolution, 1988; Agudath Israel of America, Memorandum to Members of United States Senate re Amendment to S. 2, January 3, 1992.

ment of prayer. They become officially secularized through decisions of the Supreme Court from 1948 forward, establishing, for public schools nationwide, an antiseptically irreligious regime. This regime was inevitably forced to substitute secular and utilitarian values for the values known to public education since its beginning.

But if religious schools and free parental choice are to exist, two conditions appear indispensable: (a) that freedom of parental choice be *economic* freedom of parental choice and (b) that the education chosen be free of undue governmental regulation. But it is precisely against the fulfillment of those conditions that the monopolists' pressures have been evident. On the one hand they seek to block all efforts to permit parents who choose religious schools to share in the use of tax dollars to make that choice economically meaningful. On the other they have created pressures to subject private (including religious) schools to such state controls as to render them indistinguishable from government institutions, their lives hence precarious.

We had all better focus our minds on what will result if these pressures continue to succeed. The long and short of it is that Plato's guardians will possess—body, mind, and soul—all the children of our society and mold them as "mere creatures" of a Godless state—an incalculable disaster.

Two decisions of the Supreme Court of the United States are of special significance in respect to the Guardians. One is about Catholics; the other about the Amish. The first case, *Lemon v. Kurtzman*,[13] involves the first pressure point, economically meaningful freedom of choice. The second, *Wisconsin v. Yoder*,[14] involves the second, or the freedom of religious education from rampant state power. *Lemon* and *Yoder* relate to the constitutional liberties of us all.

---

13   403 U.S. 602 (1970).
14   406 U.S. 205 (1972).

"No Popery" in New Garb

Justice to Parents: A Legislature Acts

THE DOME IS ROME'S ST. PETER'S; the foyer, the Paris Opera House. Dedicated by President Theodore Roosevelt in 1906, Pennsylvania's capitol is unmatched by that of any other state for magnificence and, perhaps, inconsistency. At various places on the sixty-two steps leading to its Ghiberti-like bronze front doors, there are, carved in granite, prayers ("May God Preserve The Constitution And This Nation"), declarations of theistic faith ("In God We Trust"), William Penn's theological claim that "Government Is Of Divine Origin," James Wilson's reminder that "Life And Liberty Are Gifts Of Heaven." [1] But the words of the 1860s' bitter champion of public education and Reconstruction, Thaddeus Stevens, also engraved there, state a view possibly inconsistent with all those invocations of the divine: "Knowledge," said Stevens, "Is The Only Foundation On Which The Republic Can Stand."

If by "knowledge" Stevens meant solely secular knowledge,[2]

---

1 As of this writing none of the granite steps have been ordered removed by any court nor any of the religious words ordered obliterated. Doubtless, due solely to oversight, these aberrations have not been litigated by ACLU or Americans United for the Separation of Church and State.

2 Which appears likely. Although Stevens was not overtly anti-religious,

the debate culminating in the capitol's ornate Senate chamber on June 12, 1968, was, in a sense, a debate between people who held religious faith to be the hope of mankind and people who held secular knowledge alone to be. It was the latter group, principally in the form of Pennsylvania's public school lobby, which had led the attack on a piece of legislation intensively campaigned for by supporters of religious schools.

The fight, in Pennsylvania's General Assembly, was over the use of public funds to support such schools. But neither of the two contending parties put it quite that way. Those who favored the legislation called it a "parental rights" bill, "enabling" legislation which would help make it financially possible for parents to exercise conscientious choice between public schools for their children and private (including religious) schools. Those who opposed the bill said that the bill was intended "to upset the historic separation of church and state in Pennsylvania" and indeed that it would "strike a death blow to the public schools."[3]

The bone of contention, House Bill 2170, was a simple enough piece. By its terms the Commonwealth would purchase, at cost, educational services, provided on nonpublic school premises, from any nonpublic school desiring to sell them, in the limited areas of mathematics, physical science, physical education, and modern foreign languages. These the bill called "secular" subjects, and the bill barred payment for courses in any of these four subjects containing "any subject matter expressing religious teaching, or the morals or forms of worship of any sect." "Nonpublic school" was defined to be a school other than a public school in which a resident of the state could legally fulfill the requirements of the Compulsory

---

it was said that his mind, "as far as his obligation to God is concerned, was a howling wilderness." (R. Korngold, *Thaddeus Stevens: A Being Darkly Wise and Rudely Great*, 10–11.) Stevens defended the common school tax in Pennsylvania over the objections of many religious groups. He was baptized by a Negro nun in a Catholic hospital on his deathbed. *Id.* at 438.

3   "Wake Up, Pennsylvania: Public Funds For Public Schools Only!" Leaflet circulated by Americans United For Separation of Church and State, May 1968.

Attendance Law. "Cost" was defined to mean the actual cost, to a nonpublic school, of providing the services (limited to teachers' salaries, textbooks, and instructional materials pertaining to the particular course). The bill stated that "no money raised for the support of the public schools of the Commonwealth shall be used in connection with the administration of this act," and the essential funding of the Act was to come, not from any appropriation, but from the proceeds of special funds (e.g., the cigarette tax). The "purchase of service" idea was an old one in the health and child-care fields. While the Pennsylvania Constitution since 1874 had barred the making of appropriations to sectarian institutions, the state's Supreme Court, in 1956, had held that public agencies in Pennsylvania could, without violation of that provision, pay public funds to religious institutions for services rendered by them in the care of dependent and neglected children.[4] The given justification: the institutions were fulfilling a public purpose. And it was deemed valuable to society that they were picking up a burden which otherwise must be borne by the taxpayers. Under purchase of service, the public did not underwrite the institutions; but its supplemental nature enabled them to carry a public burden at a fraction of what would have been the public cost. House Bill 2170 simply applied the purchase of service principle to another field relating to children—their schooling. Nonpublic schools, in 1968, were providing education to one-fourth of all school children in the state. Were the burden of the nonpublic school population to have been shifted to the public schools, the additional tax burden statewide would have come to $160 million—or to burdens unmanageable for many school districts without sizeable increases in taxes.

Yet the bill was the source of perhaps the most bitter controversy involving religious groups which Pennsylvania had seen in the past century. Because opponents of the bill had attacked it as "unconstitutional," much of the legislative debate rang with scholarly allusions to the Constitution, and many speeches from the floor of the General Assembly cited precedent U.S. Supreme Court deci-

4   *Schade v. Allegheny County Institution District*, 386 Pa. 507 (1956).

sions which conclusively proved that H. 2170 was both constitutional and unconstitutional. So much for the legalistic *form* of the
controversy. The genesis of the controversy had nothing to do with
constitutionality.

The controversy's special heat was generated by three other
factors: (1) the bill was essentially a bill for Catholics and campaigned for by Catholics (with Orthodox Jewish and some slight
Protestant support), (2) it was opposed by the public school lobby,
(3) for reasons related to both (1) and (2), it was opposed by the
Pennsylvania Council of Churches and the largest Jewish organizations in the state.

The Catholic Factor

A "Catholic campaign for a bill to aid Catholics?" Though the bill
said nothing about Catholic schools and was instead framed to
afford benefit to all nonpublic schools—schools of any denomination as well as nondenominational schools—Catholic schools represented most of the private schools in Pennsylvania. The official
statewide organization of the Catholic Church, the Pennsylvania
Catholic Conference, had supported the measure, and Catholic
citizens in the sixty-seven counties of Pennsylvania had labored
hard for its passage. The bishops of the eight Catholic dioceses of
the state were not merely wholeheartedly for it; the Catholic Church
nationally had made it plain that it believed that a principle of
"distributive justice"[5] required legislation which would provide
relief to parents who felt a conscientious obligation to send their
children to religious schools—parents who paid the public school
tax—schools which met all reasonable standards.

The American public had not always been troubled by programs
which used public funds to support the aims of particular religious
groups. From the earliest moments of the Republic, and well into
the 20th century, many schools of Protestant orientation had been

---

5   Testimony of Rev. William McManus for National Catholic Welfare
     Committee, Hearings on Federal Aid to Education, Senate Committee
     on Education and Labor, April 25, 1947.

state-supported without public stir.[6] Indeed an all-Protestant Pennsylvania General Assembly in 1839 had enacted a statute providing that public school directors could pay, out of school moneys, for the support of schools maintained by religious societies.[7] Almost no such schools at that time were Catholic or Jewish. After World War II, in accord with the heartfelt pleas of the Jewish leadership in the United States, millions in funds raised through taxation of citizens of all faiths, were sent annually to Israel without protest. Why did the Catholic plea for public aid to Catholic schools occasion a virtual crusade, first in the Pennsylvania legislature, then in the courts, to block such aid, to damn it and its sponsors as enemies of the Constitution, to appeal to the public that the Catholic drive, "imperiling public schools in Pennsylvania," was but an opening wedge to destroy both them and the Constitution nationally?[8] The answer rests partly in history.

The American nation was Protestant in origin. While its English Protestant origin itself rested, in some basic ways, upon centuries of English Catholicism, the "protest" element of its Protestantism lent it a dynamic intensely anti-Catholic. In the early 19th century hatred of the Catholic Church, preached as "No Popery" in pulpits and learned in family life,[9] became hatred of Catholics when

---

6   See generally R. J. Gobel, *Public Funds for Church and Private Schools*; W. J. Brickman, "Historical Background for Freedom in American Education" in D. D. McGarry, *Educational Freedom*, 1.

7   Act of April 12, 1838, No. 37, § 13, 1837–38 Pa. Laws 332, 336.

8   Nothing less was claimed by the opponents of House Bill 2170, either before the legislature, later in the courts (and in the media continuously over the years the legislation was in litigation).

9   Hatred of the Catholic Church, rampant in the American colonies, took particular focus in hatred of the Pope. "Antipapal feeling was attested to . . . in the everyday life of the colonies. . . . Even a game called "Break the Pope's Neck" was a popular diversion around New England firesides. School books such as the *New England Primer* were normally anti-Catholic in sentiment and were illustrated with grotesque pictures of the Pope . . ." (R. A. Billington, *The Protestant Crusade: A Study of the Origins of American Nativism*, 16.) The term "No Popery" describes less a movement than a slogan epitomizing the anti-Catholic sentiment present in the American society, repeatedly reverberating in our political,

Cartoon by Thomas Nast, circa 1875: "Foreshadowing of Coming Events in Our Public Schools" courtesy of The New York Public Library; Astor, Lenox and Tilden Foundations.

unwelcome boatloads of poverty-stricken Irish began arriving at the ports of Boston and New York after 1820. Not readily assimilable, these immigrants were deemed obnoxious cultural aliens; worse, they became a public burden in almshouses. As the century wore on, Catholics slowly found a frigid acceptance in the Protestant American society, always carefully limited by Protestant rejection of their Church and intense dislike of Catholic separateness. Catholic separateness derived from their Church's stern rejection of Protestantism, the forbidding of marriage with Protestants except upon conditions unacceptable to most Protestants, and its insistence on building its own social institutions, especially schools.

The "Catholic school aid" question which produced such con-

academic, and social life.

troversy in Pennsylvania in the 1960s, had produced violent explosions in Massachusetts, New York, and other states after 1840, and the placing of amendments in state constitutions barring public aid to sectarian institutions.[10] In 1875 the attempt was made to similarly amend the federal Constitution.[11] The debates and other public statements supporting these amendments showed an intensity of feeling against Catholics which could be explained only in terms of a deep-seated hostility to their Church and a lively fear of its resurgence in Protestant America. The popularized image of alien, ignorant, separatist hordes, subservient to a foreign monarch (the worst imaginable, the Roman Pope!), and commanded by bishops who claimed that all Methodists, Episcopalians, Lutherans, Baptists, and Presbyterians were heretics, led to the burning of an Ursuline convent at Boston in 1834 and the nativist riots at Philadelphia in 1844.[12] But the more significant effects of the image were the rearrangement of the laws to bar public aid to the schools of the despised Church and, until far later on, the widespread *de facto* exclusion of Catholics from major political office and major executive offices in businesses. For many a family, marriage to a Catholic was unthinkable (not only because of anti-Catholic sentiment but understandably with some sense of retaliation: If a Catholic would not marry a Protestant, why should a Protestant marry a Catholic?).

It is easy enough to ascribe the historic residual anti-Catholic sentiment in an older America to bigotry—that is, to malice. In the debates which surrounded the endeavors of Catholics for aid to their schools in the 1840s and in the 1960s, malice and culpable ignorance played significant roles. But sometimes left out of account

10   Protestants of the 19th century were comfortable with these restrictions—whose main aim was to bar the use of public funds for sectarian schools. Protestants were satisfied that the common, or public, school was sufficiently Protestant in character, while yet escaping the "sectarian" label.

11   See W. B. Ball, "The Blaine Amendment: New Look at an Old Bugaboo," *N.Y. Law Journal* 165, Nos. 64–76 (1972).

12   See, T. Roemer, *The Catholic Church in the United States*, 219–20; J. T. Ellis, *American Catholicism*, 62–64.

was an inherited mindset of Protestants, which caused them to see aggression in the Catholic demands, the aggression of a people whom they felt could never really be mainstreamed in the American society, people who wanted to compel Protestants to support the Catholic Church—and "Why aren't the public schools, which are good enough for us, good enough for them?"

The Public School Lobby

The organized effort of the public school lobby in Pennsylvania (which came indeed to include the tax-supported, presumably neutral Pennsylvania State Board of Education) to defeat House Bill 2170 was fueled by something comparable to a religious fervor. Understandably. After all, the public school, in the lobby's eye, was the instrument ordained by society to instruct America's children. The public education establishment in each state should be acknowledged as the supreme educational authority, and the public school respected as the superior educator. Public education was established in the laws and constitutions of every state; only by narrow exception might a child be schooled elsewhere. America required that all be taxed to maintain public education. How dangerous, it was, therefore, so the lobby reasoned, when its near monopoly was challenged and when it was asserted that the public school was *not* ordained as the sole, lawful and omnicompetent educator. Use of public funds to support one educational rival would inevitably lead to real competition, the proliferation of other educational rivals, and thus the doom of the public school. Such were the candidly stated sentiments of the public school lobbying groups which vociferously attacked House Bill 2170.

Protestant and Jewish Positions

The opposition of these forces, powerful indeed in Pennsylvania, centered on both the "Catholic factor" and on themes advanced by the public education lobby. Doubtless the opposition of the Pennsylvania Council of Churches to H. 2170 had its psychological roots in the first factor. It presented its case as one in defense of "church-state separation," with the imagery of an unhallowed union of Roman Church and American State showing not indistinctly through the constitutional rhetoric. The Council of Churches also discovered the bill to be dangerous because of its "weakening our public schools"—although use of "our" might appear anomalous in view of the fact that the Supreme Court, five years before, had rid the public schools of the last traces of traditional Protestant practices in those schools.[13] Lending force both to support of the measure and opposition to it were, respectively, the minority Jewish Orthodox community and the mainstream Jewish community (Reformed and Conservative), the latter speaking through the Pennsylvania Jewish Community Relations Council. At heavily publicized hearings by the State House Basic Education Committee, Aaron D. Twerski, speaking for Yeshiva Achei Tmimim (Orthodox), said that "the practical effect of the present situation is to tax the parent of each child that attends a religious school; this is obvious discrimination." He categorically rejected "this church-state terminology as the problem before us." I. Martin Wekselman, for the Greater Pittsburgh Chapter of American Jewish Congress, on the opposite side, said that H. 2170 "would lead to proliferated church-related education and a decline of the public schools."

The "nonpublic school aid" controversy boiled in Pennsylvania for two years. Scarcely a newspaper in any of the sixty-seven counties of the Commonwealth failed to editorialize on it. Mayors of cities, great and large, spoke out on the bill (mostly for it). The State AFL-CIO backed it strongly, while the Pennsylvania State Education Association lobbied hard against it.

Republican Governor Raymond P. Schafer had a record of hostility to "parochial school aid." Following the introduction of House Bill 2170 and a summer, in 1967, of statewide excitement over the measure, Schafer had managed its defeat by a narrow margin in the House on August 30. Representative Martin Mullen, a Philadelphia Catholic, the chief legislative crusader for the bill had, by then, built a strong and enthusiastic support for the bill in the General Assembly. His denunciation of Schafer for "causing the defeat of the bill" was echoed in the widespread reactions of

---

13   *Abington Township School District v. Schempp*, 374 U.S. 203 (1963).

Catholics and Orthodox Jews. "Why shouldn't the children have an equal opportunity to choose a religious education?" responded Rabbi Abba Leiter of Pittsburgh. By September 8, 1967, telegrams and more than 70,000 letters and postcards denouncing Schafer's action and pleading for passage of the bill had arrived at the Governor's office, the flow continuing for days with wires pouring in at the rate of 400 an hour.

It began to appear, however, that Schafer's defeat of the bill might prove a Pyrrhic victory. He deeply desired passage of a $285 million tax package, and his flouting of the ardent support for the school aid bill now loomed as a problem. The Mullen forces insisted that H. 2170 be reconsidered and taken up before final action on the Governor's tax bill. Mullen found unexpected support from a ranking Protestant Republican, Senator T. Newell Wood, who publicly urged reconsideration. On September 12 the Governor made a dramatic move. On a trade mission in West Germany, he cabled John Cardinal Krol, Archbishop of Philadelphia, seeking an early meeting with the Catholic bishops of the state to discuss the "nonpublic school aid" question. A press release stated that "the Governor is aware of the problems confronting the parochial school system and is sympathetic with them."

This adroit move sought several goals: first, to defuse the anger of the bill's supporters; second, to bring the "nonpublic school aid" question into a sort of Panmunjon tent of everlasting deliberation; thirdly, to publicly thrust responsibility for the combined "school aid" and tax package crisis upon the heads of the Catholic bishops, thus seeming to make them—and not the legislators or the millions of citizens who favored the bill—the real actors responsible for the crisis.

The Cardinal's was not the expected response. He and most of the other Pennsylvania Catholic bishops already had calendar commitments—anyhow, why was a meeting with them necessary? And indeed would not that give color to charges that a "religious war" was somehow involved? He thought that it would be well also to invite Protestants and Jews to the conference if any meeting were to be held. He expressed the "fervent hope" that the Governor's invitation "was without any of the pressure implications attributed to it by the hostile." He concluded: "Pennsylvania needs the best education for all children. It does not need religious alignment on public issues. We know you agree."

By December, Schafer did agree. Six Republican members of the House, with the Governor's concurrence, turned to support of House Bill 2170.

Justice Triumphs

On June 12, 1968, the Pennsylvania Senate by a vote of 30 to 17 passed the controversial bill (already approved by a huge majority in the Pennsylvania House). Governor Schafer, at a highly publicized signing ceremony, made the bill a Commonwealth law, now to be known as Act 109 of 1968. By the opening of 1969, an Office for Aid to Nonpublic Education had been set up to implement the Pennsylvania Nonpublic Elementary and Secondary Education Act. In January 1969 the state entered purchase of service contracts with 1,181 nonpublic schools throughout Pennsylvania. By March 1,193 schools, with a total enrollment of a half-million pupils, had sought participation in the new program. The budget estimate for this participation came to $16,833,884, or an average per pupil allocation of $31. Thus, after a two year contest, it appeared to many that the historic "religious school aid" question in America may have come to a conclusion. The 125-year contest initiated by Archbishop Hughes in the 1840s in New York, with similar breakouts in many other states in the intervening period, had been arduous. Now (fittingly in William Penn's state) legislators of all religious faiths (and from both sides of the political aisle) had enacted a solution to the problem which they judged reasonable. The democratic processes had run their course. Many considered the Pennsylvania act model legislation for the rest of the nation.

At 9:57 A.M. on June 3rd, a lawsuit was filed in the United States District Court for the Eastern District of Pennsylvania for an injunction to dismantle the new program and to have the new act declared unconstitutional as an "establishment of religion." The case would be known as *Lemon v. Kurtzman*, and the Supreme Court's opinion in the case would not only void the Pennsylvania act but become, in the decades down to the present, the great legal instrument for the enforced secularization of the national culture.

Justice Nullified: The Supreme Court Acts

Hopes and Omens

ALTHOUGH THE SUIT WAS BROUGHT against the Commonwealth of Pennsylvania, it fell to me (chiefly because of the parents involved) to argue the defense of the Act when the case came before the Supreme Court.[1] I felt confident as I approached the job. For one thing, we had won the first round of the case in the U.S. District Court where it had been brought. Indeed, that court had found our case so compelling that it had dismissed the case against us without a trial. Mainly, the precedents were on our side. In 1947 the Supreme Court, in the *Everson* case, had upheld the use of tax dollars to bus children to parochial schools, saying that no state could exclude individuals "because of their faith or lack of it, from receiving the benefits of public welfare legislation."[2] Yet it had

---

1   Defense counsel consisted of Pennsylvania's Attorney General and a team of co-counsel representing nonpublic schools, among these Villanova Law School's constitutional scholar, Professor William D. Valente, James E. Gallagher, Jr., C. Clark Hodgson, Jr., and my partner, Joseph G. Skelly.

2   *Everson v. Board of Education*, 330 U.S. 1, 16 (1947).

been in that same opinion that the Court had spelled out a hitherto unheard of interpretation of the Establishment Clause as creating an absolute "wall of separation" between church and state. Our Pennsylvania act, as "public welfare legislation," fell comfortably within the tolerances recognized in *Everson*. Then, too, in 1963 the Court in its famous decision outlawing Bible-reading and recitation of the Lord's Prayer in public schools, had set up a test which legislation would have to pass to avoid violation of the Establishment Clause: It would have to have a "secular purpose" and must not have "a primary effect advancing religion." The Pennsylvania act passed that test with flying colors. Helping children in mathematics, modern foreign languages, physical science, and physical education surely fulfilled a secular purpose and equally surely had no primary (or secondary or tertiary) effect "advancing religion." But last and best, the Supreme Court had very recently held that New York's program of lending secular textbooks to children in religious schools was squarely constitutional—a "public welfare benefit" from which children attending schools "on account of their faith" could not be excluded.[3]

It was easy, therefore, to pay little heed to warning signs which, after the fact, reveal unmistakably that within the Court a consensus was being carefully developed for the judicial destruction of any legislation going beyond busing or textbook loans which would afford major help to that vast majority of nonpublic school parents whose children attended Catholic schools. It was common knowledge that such legislation was being pushed in New York, Pennsylvania, and many other major states, and that the catalyst of this activity was the Catholic Church. The national Church was, at that time, unified, politically respected, and finding success in utilizing the democratic processes in state legislatures (and, to an extent, in Congress) in seeking economic justice in education.

The first of the warning signs had to do with something lawyers

---

3   *Board of Education v. Allen*, 392 U.S. 236 (1968). I was privileged to be co-counsel with the eminent Catholic attorney, the late Porter Chandler, who successfully argued the case.

call "standing to sue." The general idea is this: Suppose that, on the subway, I see X poke Y in the nose and that the sight of this indignity to a stranger fills me with hot indignation. If *I* try to sue X, the court will bounce my suit out, saying I have no "standing" to sue X. That's because it was not my nose that got poked. I suffered no injury. If anyone's going to sue X, Y's the lad that will have to. He's who got injured, so he has "standing" to sue. Back in the 1920s, a Mrs. Frothingham felt herself poked in the nose, not by any physical assailant, but by the U.S. government. The injury of which she complained concerned, not her nose, but her income tax payments. She came into court with the complaint that the government was spending those payments for a program she deemed unconstitutional, the Maternity Act of 1921 (for reduction of infant and maternal mortality). The Supreme Court, in 1923, held that Mrs. Frothingham had no "standing" because she could not show any direct injury to Mrs. Frothingham. The case, *Massachusetts v. Mellon*,[4] laid down the principle that taxpayers have no standing to contest how the federal government spends their tax contributions. That rule held good for forty-five years. In 1968 the Supreme Court announced a remarkable exception to the rule in the peculiar instance of a taxpayer who complained that the government's use of federal tax funds, under the Elementary and Secondary Education Act, to aid Catholic schools, violated the Establishment Clause. *Such* a taxpayer would uniquely be recognized as having standing to sue. That is to say, *the Court threw open its gates to taxpayers challenging aid to Catholic schools.*[5]

The second of the warnings come two years later in the Court's decision in *Walz v. Tax Commission*.[6] The Court's opinion in that case, though it upheld tax exemption for religious real estate, was devoted in considerable part to presenting a novel thesis which had just appeared in *Harvard Law Review*. Harvard Professor Paul Freund there warned that aid to "parochial schools" would cause

---

4   262 U.S. 447 (1923).

5   *Flast v. Cohen*, 392 U.S. 93 (1968).

6   397 U.S. 664 (1970).

improper involvements between church and state and (here was what was novel) thus violate the Establishment Clause. This second indication of possible hostility of the Court to our case, while disturbing, in no way undermined my faith in the rule of *stare decisis*—that is, that the Court would not dream of ignoring the weight of precedent. *Lemon* came on for hearing by the Court on the morning of November 8, 1972.

The Court's marshall having intoned the ancient "Oyez! Oyez!" with its prayer, "God help this honorable Court," Warren E. Burger, Chief Justice of the United States, called our case.

Most of us who approach the rostrum of the Supreme Court cannot but be conscious of the fact that the Court is an institution of vast power in a great nation, a living part of an ancient tradition, the oldest institution of its unique kind in the world. You are about to present an argument to the justices. You have staked out the points you must be sure to cover in the (usual) half hour allotted you. But your planned occasion of argument will likely soon become as much the justices' as yours in an active colloquy, styled in the 18th century, wherein what you have said and what you have failed to say may be the subject of the most intensive questioning—questioning invariably low key and courteous. This case was no exception. But early on, Justice Hugo Black's questions to me reminded me that he had once worn white robes instead of black.[7] The former Klansman seemed pruriently interested in a particular class of American female citizens, namely, *nuns*, as he questioned me:

Q. Now, "teachers" [under Act 109's terms] include whom?

A. Teachers" includes persons who are employed by the schools to teach in the schools.

Q. They may be nuns?

---

7   Black's son, Hugo Black, Jr., relates: "The Ku Klux Klan and Daddy, so far as I can tell, only had one thing in common. He suspected the Catholic Church. He used to read all of Paul Blanshard's books exposing abuse in the Catholic Church." H. Black, Jr., *My Father: A Remembrance,* 104.

> A. Indeed, your Honor, yes indeed.

Later:

> Q. Who employs these teachers?
> A. The nonpublic school employs those teachers. The nonpublic schools in Pennsylvania are Catholic; they are Protestant; they are Jewish; they are nonsectarian.
> Q. Who employs the teachers for these particular students?
> A. The school employs the teachers.
> Q. The nuns?
> A. The school.

Black had to have been familiar with the famous fact that, in those days, Catholic schools were heavily staffed with teaching sisters. His insistent inquiry with respect to "nuns" (I can still hear his slow sibilating of "*nuhns*" in his Alabama accent) seemed due to his desire to emphasize, for all to hear, that *nuns* (of all people) were actually involved in the program funded by Act 109.

Supplanting the Founding Fathers

Attorneys arguing cases before courts often "get the drift" of where the court is heading from the judges' questions. I left the Supreme Court building following oral argument in *Lemon* with no clear impression of where the justices might be heading. On June 28, the answer came. Pennsylvania's act was unconstitutional as violating the Establishment Clause. Two startling points marked the Court's opinion. First, the basis for its decision was a remarkable judicial novelty, without roots in the Constitution and invented *ad hoc* to cripple the Pennsylvania program and like exercises of presumption, whether by state legislatures or by the Congress. The novelty was Professor Freund's aforementioned entanglements notion spelled out in 1969 in *Harvard Law Review*.[8] The second startling point in the Court's opinion was its heavily anti-Catholic character. To begin with Professor Freund's invention:

---

8   82 *Harvard Law Review* (June 1969): 1680.

Freund's thesis, now to be written into the law of the land by the Supreme Court, held that the Pennsylvania program called for what he considered improper involvements between church and state. These entanglements were of two kinds (if you will bear with it), administrative and political. "Administrative" entanglements arose from the Court's belief (based solely on Freund's notions and on not a scintilla of record evidence) that, to ensure that teachers of Act 109's four secular subjects would play a strictly nonideological role, the state would have to exercise "a comprehensive, discriminating and continuing surveillance" over the religious school classroom. But teachers in religious schools—in particular, in Catholic schools—could not be trusted to play such a role. Since Catholic schools are "an integral part of the religious mission of the Catholic Church," their teachers "will inevitably experience great difficulty in remaining religiously neutral. . . . With the best of intentions such a teacher would find it hard to make a total separation between secular teaching and religious doctrine." While the Court did not assume that parochial school teachers would be unsuccessful in such an attempt, "the potential for impermissible fostering of religion is present." The Court further found "administrative" entanglements in the supposed requirement of the Act that government inspect school records to determine what part of the expenditures were attributable to secular education as opposed to religious activity in the event the nonpublic school's expenditures per pupil exceeded the comparable figures for public schools.[9]

The Court then turned to the second of Freund's notions, namely, to what it called a "broader base" of entanglement, "political" entanglement. It is important here to read and weigh the Court's message on that "broader base." Essentially, the Court said that passing legislation such as Act 109 must entail considerable political activity. Some members of the public will inevitably engage in political activity favoring the legislation, while others will engage

---

9   There was in fact no such requirement in Section 7(b) of the Act on which the Court here relied. The Act confined its payments to services which, by the Act's own definition, were secular.

in political activity opposing it. "Candidates will be forced to declare and voters to choose," and "many people confronted with issues of this kind will find their votes aligned with their faith." While "ordinarily" vigorous political debate and division are normal in a democracy, "political division along religious lines was one of the principal evils against which the First Amendment was intended to protect." And having states and communities divide on such an issue as state aid to parochial schools would tend not only to "confuse" but to "obscure" other "issues of great urgency." Political fragmentation and divisiveness along religious lines, the Court concluded, would only be aggravated by a "momentum" for such aid which might ensue from allowing it.

The Supreme Court thus selected Professor Freund to supplant James Madison and the other drafters of the Establishment Clause. Was not this choice sound? Had not Freund come forward with a formidable constitutional treatise by which to justify his thesis? Had he not, in his thesis, probed history and precedent deeply in justification of his views? To all of these questions the answer is, incredibly, no. Freund presented no treatise, cited no source in the Constitution's history, such as *The Federalist Papers* or the voluminous writings of the framers. His "political entanglements" idea had never before, in the 172 years of the Supreme Court's existence, been used as the basis for invalidating legislation. Freund's *Harvard Law Review* article was simply one law professor's personal opinion. The unscholarly genesis of our new constitutional doctrine was this: Freund, speaking from notes in a panel discussion at an ABA meeting August 4, 1968, uncorked his personal ideas opposing "state aid to parochial schools." The commercial journal of a lawbook publishing company, *Case & Comment*, widely circulated free to members of the bar, later published Freund's remarks, the cover presenting a cartoon of a fat, smiling nun, eyes downcast, taking money from a bewildered Uncle Sam. It was surprising that the prestigious *Harvard Law Review* ventured to publish Freund's remarks as a scholarly article. Their subsequent publication in the scruffy handout of *Case & Comment* was more fitting. Someone (doubtless Freund) dreamed that his remarks had multiple possibilities. Printing them in *Harvard Law Review* would give them high significance in spite of their scholarly vacuity. Thus was accom-

Public Aid to Parochial Schools

by PAUL A. FREUND/page 3

plished the transmogrification of the personal opinings of a law professor into American constitutional law.

"No Popery" in New Garb

Slavishly following the Freund prescription, the Court, in its opinion in *Lemon*, carefully avoiding the coarse vocabulary of the "No Popery" tradition, made explicit its focus on the Catholic Church as a threat to the American society.

When the Court wrote its *Lemon* opinion in 1971, much fashionable opinion conceived of the Catholic Church as an inherently dangerous force, to be treated with guarded toleration. Catholics had come into national political prominence and respect in New

Deal days. Between 1940 and 1946 Catholic, Protestant, and Jew had been forced into intimate association on shipboard, in barracks, in foxholes and hospitals, and in these situations the firmest of old prejudices of one against the another dissolved. But the post-war decades of the '50s and '60s showed liberal opinion seething with suspicion that the Catholic Menace was very much alive and must be kept confined. The Catholic hierarchy, in two decades when Stalinism was far from repudiated by much respectable journalistic opinion, was militantly anti-Communist. It likewise scandalized progressive opinion by its insistence upon the ancient Christian teaching against contraception. In the decade following World War II, Paul Blanshard's *American Freedom and Catholic Power*, an all-out attack on the Catholic Church as a lethal menace to American freedom, enjoyed huge success in the market and favorable reviews in influential newspapers and organs of opinion. Americans were being taught by many opinion-formers that the Catholic bishops wanted a Francoist America. This liberal sentiment built, of course, upon a tradition I have described earlier.

It was perhaps not surprising, then, that the Supreme Court in *Lemon* went beyond holding Pennsylvania's statute unconstitutional on the ground that the "administrative" entanglements which it presumably generated were really harmful to religion (although the religious groups which backed the Act notably failed to have discovered this harm). In the Court's essay on "political" entanglement, it did not expressly identify "the Catholic Church" as the bad actor it was describing. It employed, instead, bank-shot obliqueness, speaking of "partisans of parochial schools." Singling out these "partisans" from all other Americans who seek to exercise First Amendment freedoms in the political realm, the Court indulged the preposterous notion that that very amendment was aimed at suppressing such exercise. These particular "partisans," said the Court, would "inevitably . . . promote political action to achieve their goals." Then, of course, their opponents would, too. Now "*ordinarily*," said the Court, "political debate and division, however vigorous or even partisan, are normal and healthy [*sic*] manifestations of our democratic system of government. . ." But not when the "*partisans*" engage in such political debate. For *them* to do so is evil—so great an evil that the *First Amendment* protects against it. If you doubt that the Supreme Court of the United States could have said such a thing, let me quote the actual language (and please note the source it cited as its sole authority for its incredible conclusion): ". . . political division along religious lines was one of the principal evils against which the First Amendment was intended to protect. Freund, Comment: Public Aid to Parochial Schools, 82 Harv. L.Review 1680, 1692 (1969)."[10]

Under Freund's view, as now expanded by the Court's opinion, the effort of Catholic, Orthodox Jewish, and a few Protestant citizens to have engaged in the democratic process to achieve the passage of Act 109 was not merely evil; it was in that class of the "*principal*" evils (governmental suppression of speech, press, assembly, petition, religion) against which the First Amendment was erected as a protection.

The Court now expanded on this latter-day Founding Father's theme: The "potential for divisiveness," where religion raises its head in the political order, is a "threat to the normal political process." The Court did not pause to say what it thought the "normal" political process is. It might have been useful for the Court to have said whether the processes surrounding the elections of Andrew Jackson, Lincoln, Hoover, Hayes were, in every sense "normal" — or whether the "process" seen in myriad bizarre political developments throughout our whole municipal and state fabric are, in some sense, "normal." Also, the Court would have aided comprehension of its Freundian thinking had it been willing to say just *how* the efforts of citizens of a religious faith to pass legislation threatens the "normal" political process. The Court had, right before it, a laboratory example which, blindsighted by the Freund thesis, it refused to look at. I refer to the earlier mentioned proceedings in the Pennsylvania General Assembly with respect to Act 109. It is hard to imagine on what ground the Court could have found *that process other than utterly "normal." The voting in both House and Senate crossed lines of party, religion, sex, age, and region. One wonders how the Court could possibly have distinguished the process which*

10   *Lemon, supra,* at 622.

brought about Act 109 from that which brought about the Pennsyl-
vania Human Relations Act, the Pennsylvania Public Employees
Relations Act, or indeed thousands of measures in fifty state legis-
latures and the Congress for more than a century. The Court's
answer: It is where, and only where, religion is involved, that the
"normal political process" is threatened. Religious "partisans,"
therefore, appear cordoned off by the Court and placed in a special
class which is to be excluded from participation in normal processes—
i.e., exercise their rights of speech, press, assembly, petition, and
religion.

But it is interesting that the Court, having made it clear that the
"partisans" in this case were Catholic ("partisans of parochial
schools"), did not choose to spell out how its same constitutional
principle would apply to other religious partisans. The Israel lobby
certainly consists of, and speaks for, a religious group sincerely and
profoundly partisan in its effort to "champion" their cause and "to
promote political action to achieve their goals." The National Council
of Churches, the Southern Christian Leadership Conference, and
the United Methodist Church appear frequently in the political
arena as *religious* bodies seeking to bear religious witness through
political organization and advocacy. The causes of the Abolitionist
and Prohibition movements and the civil rights and peace movements in the '60s and '70s all involved militant political action by
religious groups. The Court, casting about for some further reason
for its baseless assertion that the "divisive political potential" of
programs such as Act 109 are so great an evil as to render them
unconstitutional, moved to an even higher level of stark arrogance:

> *To have* States or communities divide on the issues presented
> by state aid to parochial schools would tend to confuse and
> obscure other issues of great urgency. We have an expanding
> array of vexing issues, local and national, domestic and inter-
> national, to debate and divide on. It conflicts with our whole
> history and tradition *to permit* questions of the Religion Clause
> to assume such importance in our legislatures and in our
> elections that they could divert attention from the myriad issues
> and problems which confront every level of government.[11]

First, in this amazing statement is to be noticed its flat censorship
of religion. "To have" (i.e., "to allow") states and communities to

divide on the one issue of state aid to parochial schools; "to permit" questions of the Religion Clauses to assume importance: Here the Court is telling the democracy what the Court *allows* the democracy to argue about or legislate upon and what kinds of questions the people are *permitted* to make important. Second, the Court rules that the single issue of aid to parochial schools is, *as a matter of law*, one so subordinate in importance to an unnamed "array of vexing issues" that it is simply not to be considered by the people's elected representatives.

Finally, the Court engaged in prediction: If not stopped *by the Court* now, programs such as Pennsylvania's would become a "downhill thrust." This "momentum," the Court essayed—on the basis of no record facts whatsoever and on nothing but imagination—would be "difficult to retard or stop." Did the Court thus mean that if *legislatures* wanted to see such programs increased or improved, such a prospect would render legislation such as Act 109 unconstitutional? Here the Court could not bring itself to say flatly "yes"; instead it worriedly stated that "[d]evelopment by momentum" was, nevertheless, "a force to be recognized and reckoned with." Then this remarkable conclusion: "The dangers are increased by the difficulty of perceiving in advance exactly where the 'verge' of the precipice lies." In other words, since it can't be known whether or not some future legislation will go over the precipice of some guessed-at danger, even legislation which has not yet gotten to the precipice (and may therefore be considered valid) must be struck down.

Thus concluded the *Lemon* opinion. Its skewed bias against the Catholic Church would be seen as even more pronounced by the opinion the Court would hand down the same day in a case involving Catholic colleges, *Tilton v. Richardson*.[12]

---

11   *Lemon, supra,* at 622–23. (Emphasis supplied.)

12   403 U.S. 672 (1971).

Aftershocks

La Trahison des Clercs: The Tilton *Case*

TILTON HAD A CONCLUSION OPPOSITE to Lemon, government aid to religious educational institutions in *Tilton* being held constitutional. But the conclusion was opposite because the premises were opposite. Aid to religious institutions was denied in *Lemon* because the institutions on which the Court concentrated its attention were determinedly Catholic. Aid to religious institutions was allowed in *Tilton* because the institutions in that case had been willing to make departures from their Catholic mission and become secular to the extent necessary to get government aid.

Presidents of some of the most prominent Catholic colleges and universities had come to a consensus that their institutions' intense and programmed Catholicity tainted them with mediocrity. The presidents, at a 1967 conference at Land O'Lakes, Wisconsin, concluded that Catholic higher education must divorce itself from episcopal authority.[1] The Fordham Study, in the late 1960s, widely supported by the presidents, urged that the colleges take overt steps to rid themselves of vital aspects of their religious character. The

---

1   See G. A. Kelly, *Keeping the Church Catholic with John Paul II*, 72–73, 77.

motivation was twofold. First, the presidents' keen desire to "belong" might be fulfilled: They could now be acceptable to the secular academic community and government grant administrators. Their catalogues, buzzing the words "excellence" and "relevance," would show just enough of a Catholic face to attract youngsters of Catholic families but present a message to all others that they were, in fact, progressively secular. The Fordham Study program was brought to fruition in the 1971 *Tilton* case. Four Catholic colleges had received federal construction grants under the Higher Education Facilities Act of 1963. A suit brought by the famed attorney, the late Leo Pfeffer, challenged this act as violating the Establishment Clause. The United States Catholic Conference enthusiastically endorsed the defense of the aid by use of a trial scenario based, not on principles of equity and religious liberty, but of conformity to secularism. Hired to follow through on the scenario was the noted attorney, Edward Bennett Williams. Williams' biographer, Evan Thomas, describes the circumstance:

> In 1971, Williams represented a group of Catholic colleges whose federal grants were under legal challenge as a violation of the separation of church and state. Williams was asked to handle the case by the president of Fairfield College, a Jesuit institution in Connecticut, after the school had awarded Williams an honorary degree. Williams took the case, *Tilton v. Richardson*, to the Supreme Court and won. But he did not do it for free. Williams's law partner Jeremiah Collins recalled Williams pestering him after he had taken the Catholic college administrators out to lunch. "Did you set the fee? Did you set the fee?" Williams demanded. Collins had: $250,000, which he said was the largest ever charged by the firm at the time.[2]

Williams built a record on which the Supreme Court would now dwell as it handed down a victory for the colleges.

> The institutions presented evidence that there had been no religious services or worship in the federally financed facilities, that there had been no religious symbols or plaques in or on

2   E. Thomas, *The Man to See*, 239.

them . . . [t]hese buildings are indistinguishable from a typical
state university facility.

There is no evidence that religion seeps into the use of any
of these facilities. Indeed, the parties stipulated . . . that courses
at these institutions are taught according to the academic requirements intrinsic to the subject matter and the individual
teacher's concept of professional standards.[3]

Catholic higher education was profoundly altered by the *Tilton*
decision, with its potential for expansion beyond construction
grants. Its leaders would now have in hand a powerful argument
against bishops who would ask that it conform to Catholic doctrine
and worship. Further, the example of the Catholic college presidents
would prove tempting to superintendents of Catholic grade and high
schools—the idea being to conform to secular demands for the sake
of governmental aid. Perhaps the worst effect of *Tilton*, however,
was its strong reinforcement of the teaching of *Lemon*, that the
genuinely religious institution—irrespective of its value to children
and irrespective of principles of religious liberty—must be excluded from participation in governmental benefits.

Facts Don't Count: The Meek Case

While the Catholics who had pursued the secularization-for-money
scheme in *Tilton* seem not to have pursued a like proposal for
Catholic elementary and secondary schools, Catholic bishops in
Pennsylvania clung to the belief that their schools could be faith-
fully, pervasively orthodox and yet be publicly aided. A key point
in the *Lemon* decision had been that teachers in Catholic schools
would disobey a law and compulsively engage in religious indoc-
trination of children albeit in the limited area of four subjects never
taught as religious (e.g., mathematics).

The Pennsylvania General Assembly, in the wake of *Lemon*,
enacted a statute tailored to meet *Lemon*'s strictures—i.e., one
which could not be said to necessitate "excessive (church-state)
entanglements" or have a "primary effect advancing religion."

3   *Tilton, supra*, at 687.

This act provided that the Commonwealth would loan nonpublic (including religious) schools instructional equipment (e.g., projectors, recording, laboratory equipment, and other "secular, neutral, nonideological equipment" useful to the instruction of any school children) as well as non-religious instructional materials. The act also provided for state provision of inherently secular "auxiliary services" to nonpublic school children on the premises of their schools—remedial, testing, speech and hearing services. (Nothing in the act required any alteration of religious symbols, discipline, worship, or atmosphere in any school.) This act was at once challenged on Establishment Clause grounds in federal court by one Sylvia Meek, a taxpayer, and ACLU, NAACP, the Pennsylvania Jewish Community Relations Council, and Americans United for Separation of Church and State. A District Court of three judges held the act constitutional following trial. I stress "trial," because now, from the witness stand, the pat and biased assumptions of the *Lemon* Court were exploded.

You will recall that our case in *Lemon* seemed so right to the District Court that it had ruled in our favor without going through a trial. In *Lemon*, Justice White, flatly disagreeing with the majority's Freundian views, voted to send our case back to the District Court for trial. That would have allowed us to put on witnesses (including teachers) who would give the lie to the Supreme Court's bigoted factual assumptions in *Lemon*—especially the "entanglement" fiction, the need for "surveillance" to assure that teachers in Catholic schools would not engage in sly and fraudulent avoidance of legal requirements. In other words, we would substitute facts for biased presumptions. The occasion in Ms. Meek's case would now be a trial, and this opened on September 10, 1970, before the U.S. District Court at Philadelphia. Representing parents who would be beneficiaries of the new Pennsylvania law, I and our team from *Lemon* were faced by Leo Pfeffer. Leo enjoyed renown as the chief (and highly successful) courtroom antagonist of legislation to aid religious schools or parents choosing such schools. We had debated these issues throughout the country in the '60s. We would face off at last in a trial. And now the question could be answered, by live testimony from witnesses subject to cross-examination: Would a public employee, who comes on religious school premises to offer services to children inherently secular in nature, compulsively introduce religion into those services? We called nine witnesses to the stand who had been rendering services under the act to children on Catholic school premises.

Dr. William David Boesenhofer, Lutheran, with a doctorate in psychology from Lehigh:

Q. In your offering of these services in Catholic schools, have you felt any pressure to conform to Catholic or other religious views?

A. None whatsoever . . . as a member of the American Psychological Association, there are ethical standards for psychologists, and these certainly prohibit introducing any kind of religion into one's professional practice, so ethically I certainly could not . . . bootleg any religion through my work as a psychologist. . .

Pauline Stopper, speech therapist certified by the Pennsylvania Department of Public Instruction:

Q. Miss Stopper, what is your religious affiliation?

A. I am a Catholic.

Q. Is it your understanding that under Act 194 there are any restraints respecting introduction of religion in your speech therapy services?

A. Yes, I understand the legal restraints. I have sat through several meetings where we were told of those restraints.

Q. As a public employee, do you consider yourself bound to obey the laws of the Commonwealth and the State and Federal Constitutions?

A. I do.

Q. Have you introduced religious ideas, materials or subject matter into your services?

A. Not in any way.

Like testimony by professionals of various faiths ensued. We could reasonably assume that the new Pennsylvania act would be upheld. The Supreme Court would now know that its speculations about the need for religious surveillance were baseless. It would now see, in clearest light, the difference between a law professor's imaginings and reality.

The Court, failing even to mention the sworn record testimony of those witnesses, and flying in its face, said that the District Court had erred in relying "on the good faith and professionalism of the secular teachers and counselors functioning in church-related schools to ensure that a strictly nonideological posture is maintained." Further

> Whether the subject is "remedial reading," "advanced reading," or simply "reading," a teacher remains a teacher, and *the danger that religious doctrine will become intertwined with secular instruction persists*. The likelihood of *inadvertent* fostering of religion may be less in a remedial arithmetic class than in a *medieval* history seminar, but a diminished probability of impermissible conduct is not sufficient.[4]

I have italicized words in this remarkable statement. The Court, in direct contradiction of the evidence, bites its knuckles over the "danger" that the state's professionals will, by ignorance, dishonesty, or fanaticism, foster religion in purely secular matters. The "danger" is present even in a remedial math class, but—look out—in *some* schools (guess which ones) a "*medieval*" history seminar might take place, and there the danger would be of unspeakable magnitude. On this tell-tale basis, the Court, invoking Freund's homemade "excessive entanglements" doctrine, held that Pennsylvania's auxiliary services program violated the Establishment Clause.

---

4 *Meek v. Pittenger*, 421 U.S. 349, 370. (Emphasis supplied.)   Unhappily, a brief filed by the Anti-Defamation League of B'nai B'rith and four other national Jewish organizations had conveyed the same incredible message: "How can there be assurance that a teacher, teaching mathematics in a Catholic parochial school . . . will not use the rosary beads for teaching counting?" And, in respect to loans of educational equipment: ". . . such equipment can be used to construct crosses, crucifixes and altars, and it is a fair guess that in many church schools they are used, inter alia, for exactly those purposes." Thomas Nast, the anti-Catholic cartoonist of a century ago, could not have done better.

The Court also held it unconstitutional for the state to lend religious (90 percent Catholic) schools secular instructional equipment or materials for the education of young citizens attending them. If, as the Court had held in the *Allen* case four years before, secular textbooks could be loaned to children in religious schools, why not other secular instructional items? So wondered Justices Rehnquist and White, dissenting. Chief Justice Burger attacked the "crabbed attitude" of the majority. Their decision, he said, "does not simply tilt the Constitution against religion; it literally turns the Religion Clauses on their heads." He hoped that at some future date "the Court will come to a more enlightened and tolerant view of the First Amendment's guarantee of free exercise of religion thus eliminating the denial of equal protection to children in church-sponsored schools, and take a more realistic view that carefully limited aid to children is not a step toward establishing a state religion. . ."[5]

"Primary Effect," "Symbolic Unions," and Other Oddities

Burger's hopes were to be dashed. The Court proceeded not only to reaffirm *Lemon* but to expand its reach. *Lemon* became the basis, in 1985, for holding it unconstitutional for the state to allow public school children an occasion for prayer,[6] for posting the Ten Commandments on public school premises,[7] and myriad other situations in state courts in which a measure of accommodation to religious needs had been at issue. In 1989, *Lemon* became the pretext for a loosely scripted comedy known as *ACLU v. Allegheny County.*[8]

---

5   *Meek, supra,* at 386–87. A ludicrous sequel: after this, Pennsylvania enacted a new auxiliary-services statute for the providing of the services only on public school premises *or* in vans parked near the forbidden religious school premises. All over Pennsylvania you can now see these strange mobile classrooms, nonsense responding to nonsense, motorized establishments to protect us from a religious establishment.

6   *Wallace v. Jaffree,* 472 U.S. 38 (1985).

7   *Stone v. Graham,* 449 U.S. 30 (1980).

8   492 U.S. 573 (1989).

In Pittsburgh, Orthodox Jews and Catholics had each set up religious displays in public places. The Jewish display, by Chabad, a Jewish religious group, was an eighteen-foot-high Menorah, erected at taxpayers' expense, at the City-County Building. It was located next to a forty-five-foot Christmas tree, at the foot of which was a sign bearing the Mayor's name and a thirty-one-word "Salute to Liberty." The Catholic display, by the Holy Name Society, was a creche, placed at its own expense on the Grand Staircase of the Allegheny County Courthouse. Above the creche was a banner in Latin reading "Gloria in Excelsis Deo!" ACLU sued to have both removed. Brandishing the *Lemon* test, ACLU contended that each had a "primary effect advancing religion" and hence violated the Establishment Clause. The Supreme Court, by a 5-4 vote, held that indeed the creche violated the Establishment Clause, and indeed the Menorah did not. I am often nettled by liberal commentators' amused jibes at serious moral distinctions as "medieval" ponderings as to the number of angels to be found on the point of a needle. They could find a far better example of hair-splitting abstrusity in the opinion of the Supreme Court in the creche-Menorah case. Justice Blackmun, writing for the majority, made the whole thing turn on whether these physical objects sent a religious message; that depended on whether the objects were religious in character, and *that* depended on whether the "physical setting" would cause viewers to regard the objects as conveying a religious message. Since the eighteen-foot Menorah was situated next to a forty-five-foot Christmas tree (which Blackmun called a "secular" object) and the secular Mayor's secular message was at the secular tree's foot, the Menorah did not violate the Establishment Clause. Not so the creche. Away with it! *Or* (one might ask) hang a Mayor's message on it and put a secular Christmas tree next to it? *Or* (Pittsburgh being a quite secular place), amend the banner to read "Gloria in Excelsis Deo et Pittsburgh"?

The use of the *Lemon* test to ban things or acts imagined to "convey religious messages" has had other manifestations equally abstruse. By 1985 the Court had discovered a new organism in *Lemon*. It was the "symbolic union" microbe, dangerous indeed to the health of the nation. If any activity could be imagined to create a "symbolic union" of church and state, it would have a "primary effect advancing religion" and hence violate the Establishment Clause. The discoverer of this organism was Justice William Brennan, and he found its presence highly threatening in a civic project which, for nine years, had been a roaring success in Grand Rapids, Michigan. The project, serving the public, embraced secular educational courses, mostly by public school employees, at public expense, and conducted on religious (mostly Catholic) school premises. The Court held that the program to have a "primary effect advancing religion," first, because the state-paid teachers "may become involved in intentionally or inadvertently inculcating religious tenets or beliefs"; second, because "the programs may provide a *crucial symbolic link* between government and religion—thereby enlisting—at least in the eyes of impressionable youngsters—the power of government to the support of the religious denomination operating the school."[9] "*Primary effect advancing religion?*" The primary effect was in truth a civic benefit.

Once again, the Court preferred to base its decision on its own imaginings and in disregard of facts. Once again the Court simply invented constitutional law. Vague and unworkable "constitutional law" at that, constitutionality depending on subjective images deemed to fill the minds of unspecified youthful observers.

The Court, on the same day it decided the *Grand Rapids* case, shut down New York City's nineteen-year-old program under Title I of the Elementary and Secondary Education Act, of paying public employees to offer, on nonpublic school premises, supplemental educational programs[10] to educationally deprived children from low-income families. Eighty-four percent of the schools involved were Catholic, and 8 percent were Hebrew. The Court, applying *Lemon*, said that the program was alive with dangers of "subtle or overt presence of religious matter" in courses given on religious school premises. Worse, "[a]dministrative personnel of the public and parochial school system must work together" in resolving

---

9   *Grand Rapids School District v. Ball*, 473 U.S. 373, 390 (1985). (Emphasis supplied.)

10   *Aguilar v. Felton*, 473 U.S. 402 (1985).

scheduling and other administrative matters. These contaminating "frequent contacts" the Court viewed as "entangling" in every sense. The case was *Aguilar v. Felton.*

Four justices dissented from this harsh and fanciful ruling, none more vehemently than Justice Sandra Day O'Connor:

> For these children, the Court's decision is tragic. The Court deprives them of a program that offers a meaningful chance at success in life, and it does so on the untenable theory that public school-teachers (most of whom are of different faiths than their students) are likely to start teaching religion merely because they have walked across the threshold of a parochial school. I reject this theory and the analysis in Meek v Pittenger on which it is based. I cannot close my eyes to the fact that, over almost two decades, New York's public school teachers have helped thousands of impoverished parochial school-children to over-come educational disadvantages without once attempting to inculcate religion. Their praiseworthy efforts have not eroded and do not threaten the religious liberty assured by the Estab-lishment Clause.[11]

The dissents in the New York case led many to wonder whether the Court would continue to allow *Lemon* to metasticize, further damaging the fabric of freedom with biased absurdities. By the end of the Court's 1993 term, it appeared that *Lemon's* icy absolutism might be thawing in the light of realities respecting educational needs and religious liberty.

Counterpoint: Blind Bible Students and Deaf Kids

We have spoken earlier of the Supreme Court's 1947 decision that using tax dollars to provide children with transportation to religious schools did not violate the Establishment Clause and of its 1967 decision that states could constitutionally loan secular textbooks to children in religious schools. These decisions, contradicted by the *Lemon, Meek, Ball,* and *Aguilar* decisions, rested on the principle that no one can be denied, on account of her or his religion,

---

11   *Aguilar, supra,* at p. 431.

participation in a general public welfare benefit. To do that would raise religious liberty questions. In 1986 the Court had before it the case of one Larry Witters, a blind young man who had sought payments of government money for his education at Inland Empire School of the Bible, under Washington's vocational rehabilitation program. The Supreme Court of Washington had held that such payments would, under the *Lemon* test, violate the Establishment Clause as having a "primary effect advancing religion." The Supreme Court of the United States reversed. Like Byron's Julia, who, whispering "I will ne'er consent," consented, so the Court, paying verbal respect to *Lemon*, held that the state could pay Larry Witter's tuition at his bible college. Critical to the Court's reasoning was the fact that the payment was aid to an individual. Even though he would use it to support his religious education at a religious institution, it was not, in the Court's now clearer eyesight, a "direct subsidy" to that institution. Instead, it was, like the busing payments in *Everson*, a public welfare benefit "made available generally without regard to the sectarian-nonsectarian nature of the institution benefited." The Washington program created, the Court noted, no special financial incentive for students to undertake religious education.[12]

The following year there came to me the case of Jim Zobrest, born profoundly deaf, whose parents, out of deep religious conviction, had enrolled him at a Tucson, Arizona, Catholic high school. The federal-state program entitled Jim to be furnished (under the Education of the Handicapped Act) the services of a sign language interpreter by the local public school district. Again, *Lemon* was invoked—to bar this help to a disabled youngster. The school district offered Jim the service on any secular school premises but refused him the service on the premises of the one place he needed it—the excellent Catholic school where he was being educated. The School District's solicitor said that the *Lemon* test required that. I reached Arizona's Attorney General, hoping to focus his mind on

---

12   *Witters v. Washington Dept. of Services to the Blind*, 474 U.S. 481 (1986).

the sheer absurdity of his upholding denial of the service to a disabled child on grounds of church-state separation. The Attorney General said *Lemon* made him do it. Jim's impecunious parents sued. It would take six years to get the monkey of *Lemon* off the back of justice—justice to a deaf boy. The School District hired a senior partner of the major Tucson firm of Senator Dennis De-Concini to defend itself; he centered his case on *Lemon*. I was fortunate in having, as co-counsel, Tom Berning, of Southern Arizona Legal Aid, Inc. After I had flown across the country to argue Jim's case in the U.S. District Court at Tucson, the Honorable Richard M. Bilbey allowed me fifteen minutes and then invoked *Lemon* as the reason for excluding Jim from benefits intended by the Congress for "all" handicapped children. *Lemon*, at the next stage in the life of the case, was likewise the basis for the U.S. Court of Appeals' ruling against Jim—this court choosing the exotic "symbolic union" notion as its rationale. In other words, to furnish a sign language interpreter to aid a deaf boy's education in an academically excellent, but religious, school would create, in the minds of those "impressionable youngsters" dreamt of in the *Grand Rapids* case, the image of a union of church and state. And because of that, it would have a "primary effect advancing religion." Immediately after the Court of Appeals decision, I petitioned the Supreme Court to review our case.

At the level of the Supreme Court, the case attracted enormous attention. The friends and enemies of aid to parents choosing religious schools papered the Court with friend-of-the-court briefs, *Lemon* being the centerpiece of each.[13]

---

13   *In favor of the Zobrest position*: Solicitor General of the United States, Christian Legal Society, Church of Jesus Christ of Latter-Day Saints, Lutheran Church–Missouri Synod, National Association of Evangelicals, National Council of Churches of Christ, Southern Baptist Convention, Association of Christian Schools International, Family Research Council, U.S. Catholic Conference, Catholic League for Religious and Civil Rights, National Jewish Commission on Law and Public Affairs, American Jewish Congress. *Opposing the Zobrest position*: People For the American Way, National Committee for Public Education and Religious Liberty, National School Boards Association, American Civil Liberties Union, American Jewish Committee, Americans United For

On February 24, 1993, argument before the Supreme Court took place. Membership on the Court had changed since the time of *Lemon* and even since *Grand Rapids* and *Aguilar*. This bench had been described as polarized between "liberals" and "conservatives"—which description could well apply to attitudes of the justices on business regulation or labor laws but which had no relevance to the issues posed by Jim Zobrest's case. As I got into my argument, I was keenly waiting for the inevitable questioning— and whether the questions would indicate hostility or support. I opened by putting, in as simple a way that I could express it, what I felt was the gut issue in the case:

> The important issue posed by this case is whether Jim Zobrest, the petitioner, a profoundly deaf boy, would have to have forsaken education in the State-qualified religious school of his parents' conscientious choice if he were to participate in a program designed by the Congress of the United States to aid the education of all handicapped children, including children in private religious schools.

I had hoped that, while I felt there was little chance for favorable votes from Justices Blackmun and Stevens, Justices White, Scalia, and Chief Justice Rehnquist would be favorable. Justices O'Connor, Kennedy, Thomas, and Souter were on my "hopeful" list. Justice David H. Souter, a Bush appointee to the Court, soon disclosed that he shared the mindset of the authors of *Lemon*. He was concerned about the sign language interpreter's conveying "religious messages," and he stressed the importance of the *Meek* case. Our colloquy on all this eventually caused an insightful quip from Justice Byron White:

> Q. Mr. Ball, you're not really going to try to reconcile all
>   our entanglement cases, are you? (Laughter.)
> A. The answer is that I will not, Your Honor. (Laughter.)

Further laughter came when I decided to hit, head-on, the whole

---

Separation of Church and State, Anti-Defamation League of B'nai B'rith, National Association of Secondary School Teachers.

absurd "symbolic union" notion, remembering the Court of Appeals' having latched onto this as its reason for holding the interpreter services unconstitutional. Attempting humor before the Supreme Court is ill-advised, but, as Erasmus so well knew, using it to expose folly is sometimes valuable. Putting into clear light the absurdity of saying that the interpreter would be seen by Jim's "impressionable youngster" classmates as symbolizing a union of church and state, I tried to paint reality for the Court:

> I can only stretch my imagination so far, but it goes to the breaking point when I'm thinking of Jim's peers, these impressionable youngsters, saying something like "Guys, you see that fellow who's making those signs? Well, it's like awesome. Right here in chem lab we're seeing a violation of the *Establishment Clause of the First Amendment!*" (Laughter.)

At argument's end I felt fairly sure that our case had the support of Justices Scalia, White, and the Chief Justice. I now put Justices Thomas, Kennedy, and O'Connor in the hopeful column. Justices Stevens, Souter, and Blackmun would be negative.

On June 18, 1993, six years after the Zobrest parents had sought the School District's help, they won.[14] Justices Clarence Thomas and Anthony Kennedy joined with Rehnquist, Scalia, and White to produce the needed five votes. The great surprise in the opinion was the Court's total avoidance of even a reference to *Lemon*, the case which had been the heart of the opposition to the Zobrests' case, and which indeed was now the chief point in the bitter dissent of Justices Blackmun and Souter. Not to burden you with a mass of legal particulars, I think it can be said that the *Zobrest* decision, ignoring *Lemon*, moves us to new ground, crucially important to educational freedom and religious liberty. I would summarize it as follows:

> Government may afford material aid to individuals exercising a choice to be served by religious educational institutions where the individual and not the institution is the primary

---

14   *Zobrest v. Catalina Foothills School District*, 113 S.Ct. 2462 (1993).

beneficiary of that aid. The programs must provide benefits to a broad class of citizens and be religiously "neutral" (i.e., not be primarily religious in character, create no greater or broader benefits to recipients who apply their aid to religious education, and not limit the benefits in part or in whole to students at religious institutions).

The Fault, Dear Brutus. . .

The striking down of Pennsylvania's Act in 1971 did not bring about the widespread closure of religious schools which the proponents of the Act had predicted. Nevertheless Catholic schools thereafter indeed began to close rapidly. In 1994 strong efforts are being made by some Catholic bishops to vigorously promote Catholic education and to obtain programs of aid for private school parents. These would provide "vouchers" to be expended in any school of their choice, public or nonpublic (including religious). Under the reasoning of the *Zobrest* decision, a well-drafted voucher act should stand up under federal constitutional challenge.[15] Those who advocate religious schools, however, must face the fact that such schools will flourish solely on the basis of the fervor of religious adherents. Public funds will not put life into these schools but merely swing open an economic gate to them.

The steady decline in Catholic school population has been the subject of a vast amount of comment, most completely off the mark. The Catholic population in the United States did not suddenly plummet to the bottom of the economy after 1971. If anything, the general income level of Catholics after 1971, when the decline of Catholic schools began to take hold, was as good or better than their level of income in the 1950s and '60s, when they—infinitely better off than their immigrant ancestors who founded American Catholic schooling—had managed to sustain a vast number of schools throughout the nation. Indeed, during the 1950s and into the late

---

15   Proposition 174, in California, which failed of adoption in 1993, has been the most discussed "voucher" proposal. But see J. E. Coons, "Is Choice Still a Choice?" 45 *First Things*:9 (Aug.–Sept. 1994). Legislation pending in Pennsylvania gives hope for a major breakthrough for parents.

1960s, *new* Catholic schools were being built. Economics has not been the real reason for the steadily diminishing Catholic school population. Nor has the decline in female (and male) religious vocations been the essential cause. Nor has *Lemon v. Kurtzman*. Paraphrasing Cassius, a Catholic is forced to say: "The fault, dear Catholics, lies not in our laws but in ourselves." Like the leadership in many mainline Protestant churches, many Catholics of influence after the Second Vatican Council, departed from traditional beliefs, disparaged all authority but their own and embraced novelty as though it were "renewal." If there is a return, now, to a profound sense of the sacred among Catholics, to discipline, and to the careful teaching of doctrine, Catholics may have hope for a resurgence of Catholic fervor and fidelity.

Here it is important that Catholics note the strong growth of Evangelical schools beginning in the very decade of *Lemon*'s harsh ruling.[16] That growth, between 1970 and the present, reflects the intensity of religious belief of "orthodox" Evangelicals. I describe these schools later in this book. A powerful revival of orthodox Catholicism will similarly produce the enthusiasm and spirit of sacrifice which will bring a new birth of Catholic education.

Secularist pressures are increasing. The warning signals in our society are deafening, and chaos, and the Hobbesian remedies for it, loom.

---

16   Between 1979 and 1994 the number of schools of the (Evangelical) Association of Christian Schools International rose form 1,294 to 3,361, while its student enrollment rose from 220,000 to 661,475.

Criminalizing Religious Education

The Trial and Triumph of the Amish

IN SEARCH OF THE FARMSTEAD OF Jonas Yoder, I turned off from the blacktop out of New Glarus to head east on a dirt road. April 1, in southern Wisconsin, the morning was cold and dark, with heavy rain falling on old snow. The dreary aspect of the countryside matched my thoughts as to what lay ahead. I would be talking with Jonas and Wallace Miller who were to go on trial the next day but wanted as little to do with "lawyering" as possible. They were charged with having acted "against the peace and dignity of the State." They were Old Order Amishmen, the State was Wisconsin, and the crime with which each was charged was violation of a Wisconsin law which required parents to send their children to high school. Plainly Yoder and Wallace had violated that law, and plainly they would plead not guilty. Their simple point would be that God forbade them to comply. My job in court would be to translate that point into a constitutional defense.

The job would not be easy. Just a year before, the Kansas Supreme Court had ruled against Amish parents in a similar case, and the Supreme Court of the United States had refused to hear their appeal. In Ohio, Nebraska, and other states, courts had recently ruled against the Amish in education cases. In 1965 the nation witnessed the spectacle of school officials in Olwein, Iowa, physi-

Jonas Yoder, defendant in *Wisconsin v. Yoder* (1972). Ray Barth.

cally herding Amish children into buses to force them into state-prescribed education.

As I drove to the Yoder farm I thought back to what had brought me here. In the mid-1960s, William C. Lindholm, a young Lutheran pastor in East Tawas, Michigan, had become anxious, then angry, reading accounts of prosecutions of Amish in various states, with jailings and seizure of their farm animals and buggies. He knew little of these people except that they were deeply religious, peaceable to the point of nonresistance even to the rudest harassments, and lived in farm communities, separated markedly in their way of life and dress from the American culture. Lindholm began to study the Amish—who they really are, why they pursue their way of life. He also examined the kinds of offenses they had allegedly committed—with the result that he wondered greatly how it could be, in a free country, that such a people could be treated as criminals and forced, in some cases, to sell out their farms and move on to other regions as virtual refugees. He concluded that someone ought to do something to remedy the situation. Bill Lindholm became that "someone" and founded The National Committee For Amish Religious Freedom.

The National Committee came into the world with none of the eclat of the various "Emergency Committees" and "Legal Defense Funds" so prominent in pressure-group endeavors. The Committee could never have purchased the familiar full-page appeals in major newspapers or staged rallies, addressed by entertainment celebrities in prestigious halls in New York or Washington. It had no monied backers, no staff, no political connections, no glitz, no funds. Its sole asset was the dedication of Lindholm and a core group of a few sympathizers.

On Christmas Eve of 1968, I was surprised to get a phone call from Lindholm informing me of the action against Yoder and Miller in Wisconsin. They needed legal help. Amish do not sue, but Yoder and Wallace were willing to be defended. Would I take their case? I suggested an intermediate step. I would write the Wisconsin Superintendent of Public Instruction, pointing out ways by which a court case might be avoided, Wisconsin's school laws kept intact, and the Amishmen's objections stilled. Aware that the Wisconsin school attendance law exempted any child who has "legal excuse" for non-attendance, on January 20, 1969, I wrote the Superintendent, Dr. William C. Kahl, suggesting that his department could adopt a plan, similar to that successfully working in Pennsylvania since 1955, whereby a child would be deemed to have such "legal excuse" if he or she were enrolled in a so-called "home vocational school." My letter concluded:

> I do hope, therefore, that a plan can be worked out. No one is seeking to make a test case of the present prosecution, though I believe that the very peaceable defendants in question, based upon a well established claim of religious liberty, will prefer to do so than to compromise their beliefs.

Kahl's reply was a stiff-arm. Only if the Amish children were enrolled in schools affording instruction "substantially similar" to that of the public schools could they be exempted. To excuse them for any other reason would constitute religious favoritism. He concluded with a point whose significance, in terms of religious freedom, he may not have realized: that he could hold out no hope of a minority sect's being able to get the State's statutes changed to allow them exemption.

I called Bill Lindholm to say I would take the case. Joining me would be an excellent young attorney, Tom Eckerle, of Madison.

In the next weeks I experienced the joy of entering a world hitherto unfamiliar to me: that of the Anabaptists (in whose tradition, in the United States, are Amish, Mennonites, Dunkards, and Hutterites). My guide was Professor John A. Hostetler, then of Temple University, the world's leading authority on "plain people." A sociologist and anthropologist, Hostetler, originally of an Amish household, was acquainted with Amish leaders and families in the nineteen states where Amish dwell. He now led me through Amish history—their origin in 17th century Switzerland, under the inspiration of Menno Simons and Jakob Amann, who sought a return to Second Century Christianity, with the rejection of all worldly ostentation. A core Anabaptist belief centered upon the teaching of the Gospel that one must turn the other cheek and never employ force to resist evil. Hence the Amish would rather suffer persecution than take up arms in their own defense. They had experienced indeed bloody persecution in the religious states of Europe and from that had developed a profound sense of wariness of those in seats of worldly power—the men of learning and science at whose hands they had suffered and with whom they identified worldliness. And in their study of the Scriptures they had not missed Christ's words about lawyers.

Hostetler led me to Lancaster County, in Pennsylvania, where Amish have dwelled since the early 18th Century, and to Amish people whom, to this day, I treasure as friends—mild mannered, invariably good-humored, and kindly. The Wisconsin Amish, whom I was now at last to meet, had left the East ten years ago, seeking a region where they would feel less crowded by the surrounding society.

My meeting with my new clients in the Yoder kitchen was brief. Helping witnesses prepare for trial is often (and advisedly) a long process. But with these witnesses there would be little to go over. Clear of speech, but chary of words, despising voluble rationalizations, they would take little thought "how or what thing ye shall answer." In the matter of high-schooling for their children they had immovable convictions. These would come out with the sharpest clarity on the witness stand, but brief and unelaborated statements would be all that they would be supplying in their defense. They well realized that what some might deem no great offense, the State regarded very seriously. Also, they could foresee that, although being found guilty would initially occasion only the payment of a fine, they would not, because of conscience, ever pay the fine. Hence they realized that the ugly business of new fines, jailing, liens, foreclosures, and being forced to sell out and move on was what now likely lay ahead for them, their families and, doubtless soon, for all Wisconsin Amish.

But without emotion, or even comment, Jonas Yoder told me that they would come into court, they would plead Not Guilty, and they would take the stand to answer questions. I asked Yoder if he would allow his daughters (who were the "truants" in question) to be on the stand. He consented. I spoke with fifteen-year-old Frieda Yoder who would be testifying—rosy-cheeked, good natured, quiet.

Trial opened the next day in Green County Courthouse. Built of locally fashioned red brick in the 19th century, as a Romanesque landmark in a prairie town, and guarded by a statue of a soldier of the 38th Wisconsin Volunteers, this courthouse, like all old court-houses, had seen and heard her share of dreary human squabbles, occasions of tragic dramas, and joyous celebrations of justice done. Undoubtedly, too, she had heard moments of great advocacy by stars of the local bar. My Amish clients and I walked up the linoleum-covered stairway to the second floor and the main court-room, with its golden oak woodwork, eight rows of seats, and its several brightly polished brass cuspidors. We sat in that special hushed silence which always precedes the court crier's "All rise!".

The State's case would be presented by two attorneys. One was the local district attorney, but the laboring oar would be manned by State Deputy Attorney General Robert D. Martinson, a big-framed, no-nonsense type. He was sent down from Madison to assure that the peace and dignity of the state would be saved from the dangers posed by the Amish lawbreakers. I declined a jury. Local press stories unfavorable to the Amish and Amish lack of association with the general population of Green County made me feel that my clients might do as well, or better, without a jury. I felt reassured by finding the assigned judge, Roger L. Elmer, studious-seeming, equable, interested.

The State's case was quickly presented. Wisconsin law required all children through age sixteen to attend at least two years of high school. The local school district administrator, one Kenneth J. Glewen, established that the Yoder and Wallace children, of high school age, had not been in attendance at what the State defined as a high school. Having heard that Glewen had signed the truancy complaint only after the Amish had opened their own elementary school, I decided it would be worthwhile to explore this on cross-examination. This brought forth the admission that more might have been involved in the School District's actions than concern for the educational welfare of Amish children. The fact that thirty-seven Amish children had transferred from the local public grade school to the Amish school upon the latter's opening had meant a loss of $18,000 revenue to the School District. With this established, I moved to another disturbing aspect of the genesis of the case:

> Q. Mr. Glewen, you testified that you saw this Amish schoolroom. and you were in it, is that correct?
> A. Yes.
> Q. Did you at any time make any statements to the press concerning that school?
> A. Yes I think I probably did, sir.
> Q. Did you tell the newspaper, or make a statement, "I visited their school, I found a one-room building with 19th century desks, early 20th century text books, and a bunch of dirty, barefoot Amish kids."?
> A. No I don't recall, but I don't deny I did, sir.

On this note the State's case closed.

In back of the State's insistence that Amish youngsters obtain high schooling loomed visions of "delinquency"—teenagers dangerous to themselves and a prey upon the community. Public schooling would assure against this. The State's point had appeal. I decided we'd better have a closer look at the matter. It is an old maxim of trial practice that you don't ask a witness a question without being reasonably sure of how he will respond. I had taken no prior deposition of the local sheriff to find out whether Amish teenagers of Green County corresponded to the public image of "delinquent," but I felt that I knew the Amish well enough to take the risk of putting the sheriff on the stand to see whether any *facts* supported the State's broad fears. Wilbur Deininger, Undersheriff, and a veteran local policeman, testified that he was familiar with incidents of crime in Green County.

Q. You are aware that people of a religious group known as the Old Order Amish dwell in this county?

A. Yes.

Q. To your knowledge have any teenage members of this group ever been apprehended or arrested in Green County for murder?

A. No.

Q. How about burglary?

A. None.

Q. Armed robbery?

A. No.

Q. Arson?

A. No.

Q. Assault?

A. None.

Q. Possession of narcotics?

A. None.

Q. Vandalism?

A. None.

Q. Loitering?

A. None.

Q. Theft?

A. None.

Q. Reckless driving?

A. None.

Q. We hear about teenage disturbances these days, and it brings to mind our concern for young people. Now to your knowledge have any of these Amish people of high school age been engaged in any violence?

A. To my knowledge they have not.

Q. To your knowledge any persons of this group been apprehended for any felony?

A. To my knowledge they have not. . .

Q. As a Wisconsin Law Enforcement Officer charged with duties of law and order, and conscious, I am sure, of the need for peaceful communities, is it your observation that the Amish people in Green County present any threat to the community?

A. Never known of any to this community.

Of course not only were the Amish kids suspect, but indeed the Amish society. If, as the State painted it, Amish adolescents—bred in ignorance—were headed into unproductive lives, it followed the Amish community itself was a dangerous potential social burden. I thought we should not let that assumption be hidden in the case; better to bring it out in the open and test it. Ray F. Kaskey, Director of Department of Social Services for Green County, and a twenty-five-year veteran in the field of social work should have the facts.

Q. Would you say you are familiar with social conditions in Green County?

A. Yes, I feel I am.

Q. And as Director of Social Services and being familiar with conditions here, are you able to tell the court roughly how many people of the Amish group receive public assistance in this county?

A. None.

Q. Are there, to your knowledge, any Amish people in this community unemployed?

A. None I know of.

Q. As Director, are you familiar with the general breakdown in family life which is evident in many parts of our country at the present time?

A. I feel I am, yes.

Q. Are you familiar with the number, the average number of illegitimate births per year in this county?

A. Yes sir.

Q. Are any of these of Amish parents?

A. None to my knowledge.

Q. Does Green County provide any public-supported homes for the aged?

A. Yes we do.

Q. Are any Amish in such homes?

A. None I know of.

Q. Does the county provide any free service to indigent people who are physically ill, mentally ill, or alcoholics?

A. Yes.

Q. Are any Amish people beneficiaries of any such service?

A. None I know of.

Q. In your capacity as Chief of Welfare would it, or would it not, be your conclusion that the Amish people in the community do not add to the social burdens which the taxpayers of Green County have to bear?

A. I agree they do not.

Q. As to a further conclusion, would it be your opinion that the fact that the Amish children do not attend public or private full-time high schools has no effect in adding to the social burdens carried by the taxpayers of Green County?

A. I don't believe it has, no.

I now called John Hostetler to the stand. Before the court would hear the short and spare testimony of the Amish defendants, it would need the same sort of backgrounding in Amish ways and history which Hostetler had provided me and which my clients would not be able to present. Hostetler now quietly delivered the court a short course on Amish life. He told the court of the basically congregational nature of the Amish religion, its having no central headquarters, its being a "conscience group" ruled by leaders ordained by the group, the Amish abhorrence of state religion. He described their four chief beliefs: separation from worldliness, maintenance of a church community, maintenance of community rules binding on members, and a life close to the soil, "the simple life, the moderate life best expressed in rural society." I then asked Hostetler about Amish education, and his answer became of critical significance in the case:

> ... Amish, like all sub-cultures in the United States, have great concern about the values that are taught to their children, of teaching them the ultimate meaning of their faith. I would say in the case of the Amish they have very strong teachings in regard to obedience to parents, strong teachings about the value of physical work in the community, the dignity of work, the importance of work, and the goals of the Amish culture with reference to children do contrast sharply with the values that are promoted in the non-Amish society. And I think that if the Amish youth are required to attend the value system of the high school as we know it today, the church community cannot last long. It will be destroyed.

He then said that "the public school is really not equipped in curriculum and social environment to promote the values promoted in the Amish society." In particular, high schooling of any sort is rejected by the Amish:

> The objection to education beyond the elementary grades seems to me grounded in the kind of informal learning that takes place in the Amish setting versus in the high school; and certainly the environment is very different in these two places. The public school breaks down the period of isolation that is needed for personality development, etc. in the culture of the Amish. That is to say, when the teenager arrives through the 8th grade he is forming his own friendships, he is given great responsibility in the Amish society, driving horses, working in the fields, which the suburban child is not getting. He is appreciated more in the home in arriving at the age of 16, so in a sense if put in the high school he is taking a back seat in his own culture in this particular area of his life.

Martinson took Hostetler under cross-examination. His probes were several: to render dubious the Amish protest against being forced into public education by showing that other biblicist groups have no objection to public schools; to put the Amish religion itself in question by showing that the Amish could produce "no such thing as a written list of values"; to attack the sincerity of the Amish profession of the religious need for separation from the world by showing that Amish often live near, and deal with, the non-Amish world. Hostetler turned away these vigorous thrusts with gently given, informative responses. Martinson then went to ground where he evidently felt surer footing: What could possibly be objectionable in the ordinary public high school environment? Hostetler:

> The Amish, in their culture are used to learning by example—seeing older ones—while in the high school there is great emphasis put on intellectual scientific topics. The emphasis in the Amish environment is to learn how one should live. There is in fact not much time for this in the high school with the teaching of sports and sciences and fun and self distinction, which is markedly different from the environment to which the Amish belong.

Dramatic moments in trials are not only those occasional moments when the heat generated by collisions of counsel reach a point of explosion. Sometimes there is intense drama in something very quiet, like a witness' silence in the face of a critically important question. Such a moment came in the *Yoder* trial when a question from Martinson drew silence from Hostetler, who then, after perhaps half a minute, gave an answer which touched the very heart of the case. Here was the colloquy:

Q. The principal purpose to attend high school is to get education, is it not? Isn't that the primary purpose?

A. Yes, but I think there is a great deal of difference what education means—education for what?

Q. To put it bluntly, education so the child can make his or her place in the world.

A. It depends which world.

Possibly finding incomprehensible the idea that Heaven, or salvation, should be the fixed and ultimate aim of education, the state's attorney sought new ways to pose the same question, causing Hostetler simply to reinforce his remarkable answer. He was succeeded on the stand by a demure Amish youngster, fifteen-year-old Frieda Yoder. Martinson's gambit in cross-examining this witness did not pay off:

Q. So I take it then, Frieda, the only reason you are not

> going to [high] school, and did not go to school last
> September is because of your religion?
> A. Yes.
> Q. That is the only reason?
> A. Yes.
> Q. That is all.

But both the State and the witnesses for the Amish may have left wide open in the judge's mind the question of whether, giving the fullest recognition to the testimonies of the Amish and of Dr. Hostetler, Amish children, if free of enrollment in high school, would be educationally deprived.

I therefore called to the stand Dr. Donald A. Erickson, then Associate Professor of Education at the University of Chicago, today recognized as the nation's leading expert on educational effects. Erickson's testimony—devoid of familiar and empty platitudes about "excellence"—went to the heart of the issue: what is education? He attacked the notion that minority groups should have no say as to where their children should be educated. But would Amish children of high school age receive education if not made to attend high school? Erickson thought definitely so, "judging to the extent to which the vast majority of their young people are able to move in adult roles and perform them with competency." Echoing the wisdom of an older tradition, he stressed family and community life as essential to "education":

> When I look at the Amish community I see a well-functioning community.... [I]t must be due in part to their child upbringing. So I can't help but draw the conclusion because the results are so satisfactory. There is something good to be said about the process.

Public education would not be preferable for the Amish:

> I think we are learning more and more that . . . the current educational system is detached from the real world, they talk about things that they don't become involved in, for which they feel no sense of responsibility . . .

After a final brief testimony from the Amish parent Wallace Miller, we rested our defense. Returning to the court some weeks later to present oral argument, the State provided a surprise. The local district attorney, was a Mr. L. A. Koenig, an elderly gentlemen of distinguished appearance. He entered the courtroom dressed in a dark blue suit and accompanied by his wife. I could see that he deemed the occasion an unusual event in the life of the Green County Court. Koenig launched into an eloquent defense of the State's position, taking as his text the educational views of Otto von Bismarck! I am sure that Koenig felt Bismarck's philosophy of education made simple good sense. Perhaps without realizing it, Koenig, in espousing the doctrines of the Iron Chancellor, had stated the ultimate meaning of the State's position.

Judge Elmer pronounced a judgment of guilty. I believe that he had been much moved by the case for the Amish. And I am sure that the sentence he now imposed had appealed to him as Solomon-like wisdom: fines of five dollars each on Yoder and Wallace. Surely they would be happy to pay these trifling sums and be free. Most fair on the bench, and anxious to do what he deemed right, this good judge had not reckoned with the depth of conviction of my clients. They would not pay the fine: they could not because their conduct arose solely out of fidelity to God's commands.

We appealed to the Circuit Court and lost, then to the Wisconsin Supreme Court which, by a vote of four to one, reversed, handing down a strong opinion in favor of the Amish. We rejoiced, and considered the battle at last won. But we had not reckoned on the prosecutorial appetite of the Wisconsin Guardians. The State, citing the many decisions of the courts of other states against the Amish, on March 31, 1971, sought review by the Supreme Court of the United States. On May 24 that court granted review. On the afternoon of December 8 my partner, Joe Skelly, and I found ourselves at counsel table in the Supreme Court. As the always startlingly loud buzzer sounded, the marshal announced the opening of the session, and the nine justices emerged from behind the great curtain back of their chairs and were seated. Chief Justice Burger called our case. With the arguments over, one hour later, as we gathered up our papers to leave counsel table, I penned a note to Joe: "We have lost."

My prediction proved wrong. In an opinion delivered May 15, 1972, by Chief Justice Warren E. Burger and joined by Justices

Brennan, Stewart, White, Marshall, and Blackmun, the Court held that Wisconsin's action against the Amish violated the Constitution. The Guardians were handed a stinging defeat, their presumptions exposed and the objects of their criminal prosecution liberated.[1]

Important as the case was to Amish in the nineteen states where they dwell, and interesting, if not picturesque, as it was in the eyes of the public, the decision's most significant point was what lawyer's call its "standard of review," or the test it applies in determining whether some action by the state is constitutional or not. In *Lemon v. Kurtzman,* as we have seen, the Court had laid down a three-part test for determining whether governmental action violates the First Amendment's Establishment Clause. In the *Yoder* case the Court dealt with the First Amendment's clause protecting the free exercise of religion. The Free Exercise test would require courts to ask four questions in any case in which it is claimed that governmental action has injured religious liberty:

1. *Is religion really involved?*

2. *Has religious exercise been injured by governmental action?*

3. *If so, is government's action justified by some supreme societal interest (a "compelling state interest," in the Court's words)?*

4. *Even if it is, doesn't there exist some alternative, less restrictive, means by which government can accomplish its goal?*

How this test practically works out can be seen as the Court applied it in the case of the Wisconsin Amish:

1. Reviewing all the testimony, the Court had no difficulty in finding that the traditional Amish way of life was "not merely a matter of personal preference but one of deep religious conviction."

2. As to injury to Amish religious exercise posed by the State's action, the Court found that "exposing children to worldly influence in terms of attitudes, goals and values contrary to beliefs" would be destructive of the religious development of the Amish child. Further:

As the record shows, compulsory school attendance to age 16

---

1   Wisconsin v. Yoder, 406 U.S. 205 (1972).

for Amish children carries with it a very real threat of under-
mining the Amish community and religious practice as it exists
today; they must either abandon belief and be assimilated into
society at large, or be forced to migrate to some other and more
tolerant region.

3. It was the State, not the Amish, said the Court, which had the
burden of proving that a compelling state interest justified forcing
Amish children into high school. And the Court found the record
bare of such proof on the part of the State. But

> . . . this record strongly shows that the Amish community has
> been a highly successful social unit within our society even if
> apart from the conventional "mainstream." Its members are
> productive and very law-abiding members of society; they
> reject public welfare in any of its usual modern forms.

And

> There is nothing in this record to suggest that the Amish
> qualities of reliability, self-reliance, and dedication to work
> would fail to find ready markets in today's society.

Finally the Court spoke of the parental rights which
it held to be at stake in the case.

> . . . *this case involves the fundamental interest of parents, as
> contrasted with that of the State, to guide the religious future
> and education of their children. The history and culture of
> western civilization reflect a strong tradition of parental con-
> cern for the nurture and upbringing of their children. This
> primary role of the parents in the upbringing of their children
> is now established beyond debate as an enduring American
> tradition.*[2]

For eighteen years following 1972, the Supreme Court's deci-

---

2   *Id.* at 232. (Emphasis supplied.) The Court's leading liberal, Justice
     William O. Douglas, partially dissented on the view that the religious
     beliefs of the children needed to be taken into account, noting that only
     one Amish child had taken the stand. Douglas' view has been made much
     of by certain of Plato's Guardians who call themselves "child rights"
     advocates.

sion in *Wisconsin v. Yoder* was cited as precedent in innumerable lower federal court and state court opinions. Hailed by the constitutional scholar, Professor Jesse Choper, as a "high water mark" in American court decisions on religious liberty and parental rights, it has also been subject to attack. Critics of the decision have sought to diminish its precedential value by describing it as a legal curio, limited, in application, to the unique Amish cult, meaningless otherwise.

The respected legal historian, Walter Berns, of American Enterprise Institute, in an article appearing in *Harpers Magazine* shortly after the decision, said the case was poorly decided and was the first instance of the Supreme Court's holding that one can claim "exemption" from a valid criminal statute on religious grounds. In a letter which he wrote me in 1984 he said that it would have been far better had "some sort of administrative accommodation" been reached in the Wisconsin matter, adding that "behind Yoder I see Archbishop Hunthausen who doesn't want to pay his taxes." In an address Berns gave in 1980 he stated: "The plain fact of the matter is that in *Wisconsin v. Yoder*, the Amish case, the Supreme Court got itself in a position where the Amish are now an established religion of the United States."

Berns has been joined by Robert Bork in his criticism of the *Yoder* decision. Bork has attacked not only *Yoder* but also the *Pierce* decision on which *Yoder* so much rested.[3] In a 1988 address to the Catholic League for Religious and Civil Rights, Bork, paying no heed to the onward march of the Guardians, said he feared that the sort of "expansion" of constitutional religious liberty afforded the Amish by the Court would tend to "favor fringe religions and cults and to discriminate against mainline churches."

Both Berns and Bork are wrong. In its *Yoder* decision, the Supreme Court granted the Amish no "exemption" but instead recognized their right, existing in the Constitution, to educate their children according to the Amish faith. The attempts of both Bern and Bork to convert the "exemption" in Yoder to an "estab-

---

3   R. H. Bork, *The Tempting of America*, 49.

lishment" of the Amish religion is, in fact, vintage left-liberal doctrine: that if government accommodates religious exercise, it thereby violates the Establishment Clause.

We do not become liberal espousers of "judicial lawmaking" by dissenting from Berns' and Bork's arguments. Had the Court quailed in the face of the State's demand in *Yoder* on the basis of their arguments, far greater damage to the public weal would have occurred than the purely speculative damage imagined by them. To begin with, the Amish fathers (and all Amish parents similarly situated) would ultimately have been jailed, subject to repeated jailings, or forced to sell out and leave the state. But far worse: the Court would have been declaring, by clear implication, that nobody is safe from the application of any state or federal statute regardless of how patently its application in a particular circumstance violates a First Amendment guarantee. Such a rigid view of constitutionalism would have thrown Jonas Yoder and his brother Amishmen entirely upon the mercy of the Wisconsin Department of Education, which Department had already made it plain that no administrative accommodation was imaginable. Or the Amish could have lobbied for a change in the state statute—and a more ludicrous image does not occur to me at this moment. As Superintendent Kahl well noted, there was no hope that a minority sect could pull off an amendment to the Wisconsin statutes. Blind reliance upon the wisdom, knowledge and good will of legislatures to protect educational freedom is no safeguard of liberty where they are dominated by the money and power of the Guardians.

Further, how does such a Benthamite view (and it is that) of *Yoder* relate to the public interest for which the State in that case argued? The Erickson and Hostetler testimonies, coupled with those of the local sheriff and social services director, leave threadbare any claim that applying the compulsory attendance law to the Amish advanced the slightest of public interests.

Finally, does not the *highest* public interest consist in the enjoyment of First Amendment freedoms? Surely it cannot be denied here that religious liberty was *all* that *Wisconsin v. Yoder* involved.

I have a special satisfaction in having represented the Amish in the *Yoder* case. In a tiny way, I was able to help their bearing of silent witness against some aspects of what Jacques Ellul has described as *The Technological Society.* "But," you ask, "has not our modern technology produced wondrous benefits—of some of which, like penicillin, Plain People are quite willing to take advantage? And don't you romanticize these people who never fought the wars which have kept us free, labored in research labs to eliminate our diseases, or built great wealth and given it to the rest of us by endowing the arts?"

I hear your questions, and they are good. In the sense of those questions, the Amish appear of little use. But their importance is not in their utility. Their presence, instead, may tell us that utility is not the highest end of society and that, when we make it so, we seek our destruction. I well know how "useless" the Amish are, and as I think of that tonight in my house in Harrisburg, I am sure that, forty miles to the south near Gordonville, my Amish friend Joe Beiler, after working from sun-up with soil and animals, is fast and peaceably asleep. Sixteen miles to the south, down the Susquehanna River, at Three Mile Island, a new team will be at work without sleep this whole night, endeavoring to make it tidily sure that some miscalibration will not trigger an accident taking all Central Pennsylvania and half of Maryland into oblivion.[4]

---

4   For a comprehensive view of Amish life at the present, see D. B. Kraybill, *The Amish and the State.* The chapter by Elizabeth B. Place on environmental problems now facing the Amish is a striking portrayal of one aspect of the impact on them of governmentally prescribed technology.

The Persistence of the Guardians: The Evangelical School Cases

THE EVANGELICAL SCHOLAR, Frances A. Schaeffer, has described a development within American Protestantism which has grown with intensity in our century. He speaks of it as a reaction to "a fundamental change in the overall way people think of and view life and the world as a whole"—a shift toward "a world view based on the idea that the final reality is impersonal matter or energy shaped into its present form by impersonal chance."[1] Revulsion toward the shift became manifest in the 1890s when a group of scholars from old line schools (e.g., Princeton) published a series of five paperback volumes setting forth what they deemed to be "the fundamentals" of the Christian faith. In 1920 Dr. Curtis Laws coined the term "fundamentalist" to describe those who professed five points of doctrine—the inerrancy of the Bible, the Virgin birth, the substitutionary atonement, the Resurrection, and the Second Coming of Christ in the flesh.[2] Many Evangelical Protestants who did not identify themselves as "fundamentalists" shared both the revulsion and those beliefs—especially after the Supreme Court's

---

1   F. A. Schaeffer, *A Christian Manifesto*, 17–18.

2   A. P. Stokes, *Church and State in the United States*, 592.

1963 decision barring Bible-reading in the public schools and their ensuing totally irreligious environment. Out of these streams of conviction among Protestants emerged, almost imperceptively at first, schools called "Christian schools" by their supporters. By 1975, these were being established at the rate of three a day nationally. Until then when one thought of Christian religious schools, one thought mainly of the numerous Roman Catholic schools. The new Protestant Christian schools (Evangelical or fundamentalist) were founded out of the same motivation which had caused Catholics to found their schools: the profoundly felt need to provide their children with a totally religious education (coupled with certainty that a child's eternal salvation would be risked by placing the child in public school). Behind that—for those Catholics, and now for the new Protestant school founders—lay a dual conviction: that their faith was the one true faith; that that faith was the most important thing in their lives. As with the Catholics before them, the Evangelicals and fundamentalists were willing to make great personal sacrifices to assure a Christian education for their children. Joining in the Catholic sacrificial effort were persons of religious vocation, especially nuns, who gave their lives to generations of children. To join in the new Protestant school effort came likewise teachers in religious vocations—lay teachers, at low pay, ardent in zeal.

It was inevitable that the new Christian schools would come to the attention of public school authorities, who, in most states, are charged with responsibility for enforcing the truancy laws or are awarded some limited controls over nonpublic schools, or in some states, *carte blanche* control over their entire educational process.

In 1975 the first of a series of collisions between state public educational authorities and the Protestant schools came into the courts. Most of these cases provided a sharp and inclusive picture of what has been involved in a spreading conflict between church and state in education—a conflict which, at this writing, is far from being resolved. The remarkable feature of these cases was that they put into focus, in a way never as fully seen in American courts, the ultimate educational questions: What is education? May the state define it and, if so, to what extent? What is rightfully the power of the state with respect to the education of children? What are the rights of parents in the schooling of their children? What is the scope of religious liberty in the education of the young? At the time of the emergence of the new Evangelical school movement, the population of the Catholic schools was starting to decline. They and the Lutheran schools already enjoyed a sort of "grandfathered-in" public status and had rarely felt called upon to question state regulatory requirements.

With the Protestant newcomers it was different. To the public educational establishment, they were an unknown. Some in the establishment were plainly alarmed that these schools meant a growth of rivals in the education market. Since they were not schools of mainline churches and were, in part indeed, fundamentalist, their appearance was greeted with lively official suspicion. Viewed as upstarts, they were proving troublesome, questioning state regulatory requirements which either had never been questioned by the established religious schools or had not been enforced against them.

In Kentucky, in 1977, came a train of events in which each of these "ultimate" questions would not only be posed, but posed dramatically, and not only posed dramatically, but answered.

The setting was a lovely old American town, Frankfort, Kentucky's capitol. Established by the Virginia legislature two centuries before, when the Bill of Rights was in gestation, Frankfort played its role in the early development of Americans' constitutional liberties. It was the birthplace of the Kentucky Constitution, a document which, as this chapter will show, is far from being a dead letter today. Frankfort has an "old town" section, a square mile nestled in a crook of the Kentucky River. There, on St. Clair Street, stands the Franklin County Courthouse, an ancient Greek-revival style building. On its steps, on a June morning in 1977, was gathered a small crowd of people, mostly young, some with children clinging to them. A man they called a "preacher" led them in a short prayer. The preacher asked God's help that "His Honor, the judge, and our attorney, and the men in the state government, will be guided by Thee to do what is right." Heads bowed, hands joined. Faces reflected anxiety and hope, fear and quiet resolve. The courthouse door was unlocked, and they were guided to Courtroom No. 1, of the Franklin Circuit Court, Hon. Henry Meigs presiding. Trial in the case of *Rudasill v. Kentucky State Board of Education* was about to begin.

This event, which was a supreme crisis in the lives of the parents in Courtroom 1, was the culmination of a controversy which had had its start early in 1977. Kentucky public school officials, seized with a growing sense of alarm that new private Evangelical schools were suddenly being founded, on August 30 had sent them warnings that they must be licensed by the State or cease to operate. Parents enrolling their children there would be prosecuted for truancy. Pastors of the churches operating these (non-tax-supported, racially nondiscriminatory) schools had told the State that the schools' authority to exist derived from the churches which had founded them—not from the State. Limited, "common good" regulation, yes; licensing, no. This church-state collision soon became highly publicized. Nicholas von Hoffman, on CBS radio, July 21st, noted that many of the Kentucky Christian schools employed an educational program whereby children study primarily by themselves, engaging in reading and writing in a sort of "continuous examination system," with teachers playing more of the role of tutors in the Socratic sense. Said von Hoffman, of the Kentucky public school officials:

> . . . the authorities are disturbed because the children teach themselves. Never mind that every school teacher since Socrates has maintained that that is the only way to learn. I've reminded Socrates that he isn't accredited in the State of Kentucky.

The two Louisville newspapers, *The Courier-Journal* and *The Louisville Times*, each edited and published by the same individual, by the summer of 1977, had taken it upon themselves to pronounce judgment in the controversy. In its editorial of July 14, 1977, the former, taking aim at the Kentucky Christian schools, sternly warned against teaching which was not "conventional teaching," that if private schools are to operate they must use "state-approved textbooks," that while "[a]dvocates of unregulated private schools as a substitute for public education have a right to argue," "the state has a duty to stand firm." The *Courier-Journal* quoted approvingly the statement on the Kentucky Christian schools, of Rev. Bob Brown, Chairman of the Kentucky State Board of Education:

> The teachers are not qualified, the facilities are inadequate, they don't use books on the State list, and . . . they teach that everything in the Bible is literally true from Genesis all the way through.

Brown, the education czar of the Commonwealth, who passionately argued for his belief in church-state separation, was a Baptist minister who, in his role of secular power, did not drop "Reverend" as his preferred mode of being addressed. Thus the State Board, through its spokesman, made it clear that no child should read books not licensed by the State to be read and raised the question whether any school might teach religious views not sanctioned by the State. "Teachers not qualified"? As Chesterton had asked of the eugenicists of the early 19th century who had argued for "sterilization of the unfit," "Unfit for what?" so one might have asked in reference to teachers: "Qualified for what?"

In August, with their school terms about to begin, the schools sought my help. I advised the pastors to seek a meeting with Kentucky Governor Julian Carroll in hopes of securing his willingness to ask the State Board of Education to slow down its now evident threat to force closure of the Christian schools. Carroll retorted that the pastors' plea was a "crusade for ideology" and said that such crusades "are just a bunch of crap." Religious schools, he said, must be subject to the same regulations as public schools.

Help at the highest level blocked, I continued to believe that state enforcement proceedings, prosecutions of parents, or shut-downs of the schools could be avoided. I hence sought a meeting with Kentucky's Attorney General. His reaction to the pastors' plea was a three-pronged directive: (1) any child enrolled in an "unaccredited" [unlicensed] school should be considered truant, and local public school boards should accordingly then "take appropriate action," (i.e., criminal truancy prosecutions), (2) parents of such children would have one week to transfer them to the public schools, (3) if their mode of schooling was not at once dropped by any school using it, that school would be closed.

This hip-shooting was based on no *evidence* whatever. Not one fact had been garnered by the State as to any particular Christian school—whether it was located in a good facility, what its curriculum was, and, above all, what results it was managing to produce educationally. All the "evidence" about the Christian schools which the Attorney General possessed appeared to have been borrowed from the speculations of the Reverend Bob Brown. Nor did the directive take into any account the specific objections which the schools had voiced to particular State regulations—for example, the requirement that only state-dictated textbooks—none other—could be used in any of the schools. One more try was needed. It was intolerable that good private schools (in this day when literacy and virtue are so greatly needed in our country) could be rubbed out by an unthinking ukase and that parents' religious enterprises would be thoughtlessly destroyed. We hence sought a meeting with the State Board of Education. The meeting took place on September 9. What took place can only be described as bizarre.

We assembled around a conference table in the spacious boardroom of the twenty-six-story Capital Plaza Tower. With me were co-counsel, Louisville attorney Ted Amshoff—Catholic, young, and very gifted—and four pastors. With the Reverend Brown was a brace of State attorneys, educational officials, and—here was the bizarre element—a bank of television cameras from local TV stations, and a brace of reporters. Reverend Brown had made the meeting conditional upon the inclusion of these. But we had sought the meeting for serious purposes. The pastors had felt it a vitally important chance at last to "make their case"—to talk freely and candidly about educational processes, children's needs, the State textbook and teacher qualifications, and school licensing problems. And it would seemingly be the State's agenda to speak with equal freedom and candor as to why the State Board and the Attorney General had taken the positions they had—and indeed also to speak of educational processes and children's needs. Why, then, floodlights and television cameras, media representatives crowding about the 10 x 4 conference table? But one answer suggested itself: The pastors were to be "shown up"—shown up as rednecks, ignorant fanatics daring to question the public educational establishment. Unhappily for Brown & Co. my clients were not able to play their presumed redneck role. That was because they were people of dignity, intelligence, and graceful bearing. The State folk should have caught that early in the conversation which now ensued, but blinded by their preconceptions, they played out to the end the scenario they had scripted.

The show was soon over. Brown's media exposé had backfired. But we had had no meaningful hearing. Seven days after that the State Department of Education ordered local school districts to start legal proceedings against all parents having a child enrolled in a non-licensed private school. Some districts took this as a warrant also to move with criminal proceedings against pastors. For the parents, it was time to counter-punch. Thirty-two parents, joined by five pastors, now brought suit against the Kentucky State Board of Elementary and Secondary Education, claiming that to apply the State's licensing scheme to their schools would violate their religious liberty. The trial which ensued, drawing national attention, provided many in the country a look at presumptuousness and ruthlessness on the part of the public education establishment of a major state.

Kentucky is not a wealthy state. Though its Attorney General's office was well staffed, the Kentucky Guardians decided, regardless of the cost to taxpayers, to hire Special Counsel for their defense in the case. That was odd. My clients' suit did not attack the public schools. Why the extravagance of this move by the State Board? For one reason: to bring to heel any private religious school which questioned the educational supremacy of the state. The Special Counsel chosen was Burt T. Combs, senior partner of the Louisville megafirm of Tarrant, Combs & Bullitt, formerly a United States Court of Appeals judge, formerly Governor of Kentucky. He had also, when governor, appointed Henry Meigs as judge—the judge who would now preside in *Rudasill v. Kentucky State Board of Education*!

Trial opened June 14, 1978. After a year's harassment of parents by state officials for having enrolled their children in "inadequate" schools, trial was welcome. Trial would open up all sorts of possibilities—not only to showcase the schools but also to explore the minds and competence of those who sought to regulate them. We would be eager to put our parents, pastors, and kids on the stand

and let the State have at them. But we were equally eager to bring the Guardians to the stand. As our little crowd settled into seats in Courtroom 1, I was suddenly reminded that here, at Frankfort, Kentucky, a scene was being reenacted such as Catholics in France had faced at the start of the twentieth century with the imposing of the Association and Separation laws[3] and Catholics in Germany in the 1870s as the *Kulturkampf* was begun.[4] Thinking of these it was obvious that *our* trial in the America of 1978 would need to center on four clusters of evidence: evidence as to what education is, as to who may teach children, as to whether the state is the ultimate educator, and as to what is the meaning of a religious role in education.

As plaintiffs in the case, we were entitled to open. The pastors established that, as ministers of the Gospel, they were charged with the duty to bear witness to the Lord and further the mission of their churches by creating Christian schools. Those schools were deemed to be a *ministries* of the church, integral parts of its religious mission. But for that mission the schools would not exist. Christian teaching (under Matthew 28:18–20) was to permeate every aspect of the school and the child's life. Prophet-like in appearance, the theologian Rousas John Rushdoony, stressed the levitical ministry of the schools. It was thought essential that children be kept in an environment conducive to the faith in their formative years and that they be trained in good manners, modesty in dress and grooming, respect for one another and for civil and parental authority. As the picture of the schools gradually emerged through the testimony of parents, pastors, and school children, it was also borne home that incidence of use of drugs or alcohol, of stealing, vandalism, or cheating were virtually nonexistent in the schools; further, that an atmosphere of love characterized them; and that they pursued close student-teacher relationships.

That picture was not disturbed by the lengthy cross- examination pursued by Burt T. Combs. His first aim was to score a knockout

---

3   See R. M. Healey, *The French Achievement*, 23.

4   See C. J. H. Hayes, *A Generation of Materialism*, 86–87.

by showing that the religious claims of the pastors and parents was bogus. The churches belonged to no known national denomination. Was anyone's religious liberty really threatened? But his highly aggressive attempts to overpower the witnesses and to push them into contradictions backfired. The "fanatic" pastors, the "redneck" parents seemingly misled by them, and the children of the Christian schools' thralldom yielded him the opposite of what he sought. The parents—capable, mature-seeming individuals—testified to financial sacrifices which they made in order to educate their children in the schools. A plaintiff parent, Larry Lambrich, stated that his total family income for 1977 had been $16,000, out of which he supported a five-member family and paid $1,200 a year as tuition for three children at Owensboro Christian Academy. After the trial Judge Meigs would describe the parents' testimony as "radiant."

To refer back now to the four-part test which, in *Yoder*, the Supreme Court had said must be met when someone claims that government is violating religious liberty, our case had now passed the first part: Religion was central to my clients' case. The whole idea of founding the schools was religious, the supreme motivation of the parents was religious, and the schools were pervasively religious. Would the State's intended closure of the schools and its prosecution of pastors and parents create injury to religious liberty? The trial would now shift to that second part of the *Yoder* test. At the same time it would explore whether, if such injury was threatened, the State could nevertheless show that a "compelling state interest" justified the State's actions.

The State based its case on a simple enough proposition: It is in the public interest that all children receive good education; only schools approved by the State can provide that; therefore all schools must be state-approved (licensed). Locked up in the proposition was, of course, the meaning of "good education" and what might be involved in a school's getting approved. Though it was likely that the Guardians would expand on the first, the only effort to define the critical question of what "good education" means would be the ample testimony of the Christian school administrators and parents.

On the stand, the pastors, principals, and teachers from the schools established the educational character of the schools. The schools taught the "basics"—traditional branches of learning—for a term of 180 days of six hours. They met all fire, safety, sanitation, and immunization requirements of law and reported attendance to the proper civil authorities. Employing nationally standardized self-executing achievement tests such as the California Achievement Test (reading, math comprehension, etc.), the schools produced profiles of test results showing that their students were exceeding the national norm. Parents testified to their strong satisfaction with the education their children were getting in the schools and their confidence in an educational free market.

The State's avoiding any attempt to define "good education" was due to its view that there was no need to waste time with that. The State, right there at hand, had the key to good education. That key was the State's approval system: A school which followed the State's regulations, and thus won "approval," would therefore inevitably provide good education. The regulations, then, became the second major focus of the trial. For two reasons the picture disclosed of Kentucky's regulations has an importance going far beyond the Kentucky case. By their calculated looseness of language, they typified the Orwellian character of governmental regulation today in many areas other than education. "Orwellian" is not an overstatement. The Supreme Court, in earlier cases, had pointed out that governmental regulations affecting First Amendment freedoms must be drawn with "narrow specificity." A loosely worded regulation as to which "men of common intelligence must necessarily guess at its meaning and differ as to its application" is a "highly efficient *in terrorem* mechanism" especially to "those with a conscientious and scrupulous regard" for the law.[5] Here are some samples of the Guardians' regulations in Kentucky:

- Section IV of the State's Standards for Accreditation set the following as a standard which the schools, on pain of "disapproval," were bidden to obey:

Curriculum, objectives, decision, and implementation should

---

5   *Keyishian v. Board of Regents*, 384 U.S. 589, 599, 601, 604 (1967).

be characterized by unit balance and articulation with the schools below and above it, while retaining program flexibility.

The Guardians' witnesses were unable to say what that meant. The pastors found it incomprehensible.

- Standard VII expressed the State's idea of safeguards a school would need to observe in order to provide quality education (or else be disapproved):

> Major safeguards for quality education are a well- designed master schedule, effective administrative routines, adequate undisturbed class time, and *profusion for a high degree of self-direction on the part of students.* (Emphasis supplied.)

No witness was able to explain what the "profusion" business was all about or to account for the State educators' lapse in English usage.

Did you catch sight, in that "standard," of the use of the verb "are"? Focus on it. It's a new regulatory style now widely employed in the fields, not only of education, but of health, environment, and trade. It employs phrases which merely describe a seemingly desirable state of things (like "All members of the faculty hold bachelors' degrees" or, as here, "Major safeguards for quality education *are* . . . (etc.)"). Since the Kentucky regulations had much such mild and purportedly non-threatening language, I felt we should get the Guardians to tell the court whether the words following "are," in the above standard, were in fact intended to be requirements. A State witness, in hesitant response, tried to shift the discussion to other (and highly interesting) grounds. Seeking to portray the State as benign in its regulations, he said that the State administered them according to its subjective estimates of the "intent" of the school, a personal judgment as to whether the school was "making a good faith effort" to comply. Thus many of the "standards," with such "descriptive" wording, were really blank checks which the Guardians were free to fill in as they pleased, open commissions to roving State inspectors to "approve" or deny "approval" according to their personal inclinations.

In view of that, the pastors and parents not unnaturally wondered which of the myriad regulations (always described by the State as "minimum" standards) the State regarded as binding law. If any one of them, cast in mandatory terms, was not so regarded by the State, then why should any other of the standards be regarded as

"law"? I thought it would be worthwhile to explore this with the State's chief of accreditation, one William L. Hampton:

> Q. If I asked how many failures would result in denial of approval, what would your answer be?
> A. Are you speaking of percentage-wise?
> Q. I'm talking only about the "shalls."
> A. Well, I'd say thirty or forty percent.
> Q. How do you come by that answer?
> A. Well, that's just off the top of my head.

Out of the miasma of the regulatory mass, some requirements, absolutely unacceptable to the pastors and parents, emerged clearly. The State had laid it down that private religious schools must use only textbooks selected by a state textbook commission (a body consisting of nine public school officials). Any school not satisfied with a book on the commission's list would have to go through a procedure with the commission to get an exception. Like the State's "approval" power, the commission's power was a blank check to State officials, upon which they could designate any book according to the subjective philosophy, values, tastes and literary insights of the nine individuals.

A second requirement pertained to curriculum. The unlimited "approval" power assumed by the State officials embraced the power to set the curriculum of all private religious schools. In addition, the standards specifically provided that *all* private schools must teach "consumer education," a provision which the pastors and parents believed to import emphasis on materialism. They likewise objected to the requirement of a separate "functional program of guidance services," since the schools integrated "guidance" into the whole life of the school, and that guidance was biblically directed. The State said that required curricular offerings could be omitted only if "local surveys of community needs" indicated this. The pastors said they would not resort to community surveys in order to determine their offerings.

Finally, there was the requirement that only teachers qualified by the State could teach in the schools. The State failed to produce any evidence of scholarly research showing that state teacher certification produces teacher competence or that, due to teacher certification, public schools were producing excellence in education. The State, however, insisted that a bachelor's degree was a necessary condition of teacher certification. But we showed that a bachelor's degree in Kentucky could be obtained at a State-supported university in such subjects as hotel-motel management, restaurant management, or recreation. It was brought home to the court that forty states and the District of Columbia did not require private school teachers to be state-certified.

The trial concluded, with closing arguments taking place August 14. On October 4 Judge Meigs ruled in favor of the parents and pastors. He characterized the State's approval scheme as "dubious" and its action as "poorly conceived, ill-defined and quite direct interference with plaintiffs' religious liberty." Resorting to the *Yoder* test, he found no evidence that the State had a "compelling state interest" in imposing the "turgid rhetoric" of the standards on the Christian schools. He concluded by going beyond a stirring defense of the State's intended victims in order to speak with remarkable candor about the Guardians:

> The State is unable to demonstrate that its regulatory scheme applied to the *public* schools had any reasonable relationship to the supposed objective of advancing educational quality; not only is that unfortunate truth apparent in this case, but more ominously, it has become apparent to the taxpaying Kentucky citizens who support the educational apparatus. Plaintiffs, on the other hand, have shown that without benefit of the State's ministrations their educational product is at least equal to if not somewhat better than that of the public schools, in pure secular competence.

The Guardians now hastened to the Supreme Court of Kentucky. Friend-of-the-court briefs supporting them came from the expected supporters of the Guardianship—the Kentucky Association of School Administrators, State Education Association, and School Boards Association—while on our side were Seventh-day Adventists, Lutherans, and a lay Catholic organization. (The superintendent of schools of the Archdiocese of Louisville had supplied an affidavit in support of the State's case.) The Kentucky Supreme Court, deciding in favor of the schools, did two surprising things: it handed down its decision within three weeks, and it based its decision not upon the First Amendment but upon an ancient provision of the Commonwealth of Kentucky (its Section 5): ". . . no man shall be compelled to send his child to any school to which he may be conscientiously opposed." A Catholic, Justice Robert O. Lukowsky, wrote the opinion upholding fundamental rights under that provision.[6] Concentration on the meaning of "conscientiously" permeated his opinion. Like Judge Meigs, he took occasion to rap the knuckles of the Guardians:

> To say that one may not be compelled to send a child to a public school but that the state may determine the basic texts to be used in private and parochial schools is but to require that the same hay be fed in the field as is fed in the barn. Section 5 protects a diversified diet.

The Guardians, however, like the Guardians in *Yoder*, had not exhausted their anxious quest for power. They took their case to the Supreme Court of the United States. There the significance of Section 5 caught up with them. It is the general rule that the U.S. Supreme Court will not review a final ruling by the highest court of a state interpreting a provision of its state's constitution. On May 12, 1979, the U.S. Supreme Court refused to hear Kentucky's case. There was rejoicing that night in churches in Owensboro, Paducah, Louisville, Frankfort, and Somerset. The spirit of liberty generated by *Yoder* had moved on to aid the Kentucky parents and religious freedom. Similarly it did, in like Evangelical school cases in Vermont, Ohio, and Maine.[7] The wave would be turned back by courts

---

6   *Kentucky State Board of Education v. Rudasill*, 589 S.W.2d 877 (1979).

7   The Maine case (in which our partner Philip Murren served with me as co-counsel) involved the state's effort to shut down eighteen Evangelical schools. Though Maine is not an affluent state, it spent money lavishly upon its prosecutorial effort, employing three nationally recognized educational experts—George Madaus of Boston College, Kevin Ryan of Boston University, and Joseph Cronin, former State Superintendent of Education of Illinois. They expounded educational theory exquisitely.

in similar cases in Nebraska, South Dakota, Massachusetts,[8] and Michigan. There the Guardians prevailed. In 1994, due to the continuing claims of the public education establishment in many states, but also to other factors, the future of private religious education and parental choice is far from assured. One of those other factors was vividly seen in the matter I now take up.

All, on cross-examination, admitted that they had never visited one of the prosecuted schools. We brought on to the stand Donald Erickson, whose testimony in the *Yoder* case had been so effective. Erickson, in short order, turned the case from the world of theory to the world of reality. He satisfied the court with his highly practical contention that the *prescriptions* of the theorist-Guardians are not what counts. The test should be: *Did education happen?* Why put schools out of business, he argued, in which basic education is provably happening? Merely for their failure to obey the prescriptions of a failing public school system?

8   In the Massachusetts case, *New Life Baptist Church Academy, et al. v. Town of East Longmeadow, et al.*, 885 F.2d 940 (1989), Judge Stephen G. Breyer (now Associate Justice, United States Supreme Court), wrote a solidly pro-Guardian opinion, which, purporting to cite all prior relevant cases, omitted any reference to the *Rudasill* case.

Elephants, Orangutans, and the Cardinal

THE "GUARDIANS" IN THE CASES we have been discussing are the organs and agents of the public school establishment. But there are other governmental bodies which seek control of private education—even religious private education. Sometimes their actions are deliberate; they directly target religious institutions. But major state agencies (and especially federal agencies) today are elephantine in size, and the heavy feet of these bumbling giants sometimes—all unaware—trample gardens. The distance between the elephant's huge foot and—way up there—his small brain, may be too great for him to avoid taking inadvertent steps.

The odd case which arose in Philadelphia in 1976 concerned a governmental elephant lifting its foot above someone's well-tended garden, and the owner's desperate effort to move the beast off before the garden was obliterated.

The elephant was the National Labor Relations Board. The garden was a cluster of parish elementary schools in the Catholic Archdiocese of Philadelphia. The desperate effort took place in the U.S. District Court for the Eastern District of Pennsylvania. Unionism (or at least a union) had entered the Catholic schools of Philadelphia in 1968. The relationship between the Archdiocese and the Association of Catholic Teachers, Local 1776, had not always been tranquil. It became strained to the extreme when, on January 16, 1976, the Association filed a petition with the National Labor Relations Board (NLRB) asking the Board to certify it as the "exclusive bargaining representative" for all 2,000 lay teachers in the 273 parish elementary schools located within the Archdiocese. Acting under the National Labor Relations Act, Mr. Peter Hirsch, Regional Director of NLRB, responded by dispatching a set of orders to John Cardinal Krol, Archbishop of Philadelphia—forms which the Cardinal was expected to fill out—and soon, since a "hearing" on the matter would be held February 23rd. The Cardinal was addressed as "the employer representative to contact"; he would be allowed to be represented by counsel. But immediately he was to fill out a questionnaire which bade him "indicate with a 'X' classification (2) which best describe(s) your business":

(a) Processing and/or manufacturing ....
(b) Wholesaling ....
(c) Retail outlet ....
(d) Trucking ....
(e) Service Organization ....
(f) Public Utility or Transit System ....
(g) Newspaper and/or Broadcasting Station ....
(h) Other .... describe ....
....

Describe briefly the nature of your business, also state whether it is one of a chain or one of several separate but related enterprises:
....

During the past calendar fiscal year:
(a) Did dollar volume of your sales or performance of services to customers outside the State equal or exceed $50,000? Yes ( ) No ( )

NLRB also enclosed a notice to the teachers which the Archbishop was told to post in the parish schools.

The letter to Cardinal Krol went further. It sought "copies of correspondence . . . covering any of the employees," and an "alphabetized list" of them "together with their job classifications for the payroll period immediately preceding the date of these letters." It concluded by stating that an "investigation" was to ensue. The Cardinal was warned against making any false state-ment, since if he did so willfully, he could be punished by fine or imprisonment.

Was this an example of the bumbling elephant, the governmental giant inadvertently lurching into a place it didn't belong? Maybe. Under the terms of the National Labor Relations Act an "employer" is simply somebody who employs people. The lay teachers in the parish schools were obviously employees. The black print of the act made no exceptions for employees in religious schools, or their employers. So why shouldn't NLRB have gone ahead? Why should these church schools be treated differently from any other employ-ers? Perhaps because an act designed by Congress to prevent "industrial strife and unrest" was being applied by the government of the United States to a religious ministry. Perhaps because, only five years before, the Supreme Court, in the *Lemon* case, had described the Catholic schools as just that, an "integral part of the religious mission of the Catholic Church." Perhaps because NLRB should not be treating church organisms as it would a steel mill, chain stores, or a plastics factory.

No, here was not the inadvertent action of a clumsy monster. The NLRB officials were acutely aware of the nature of the schools (and of whether the schools were "businesses" or had "sales" yielding a "dollar volume"). NLRB knew exactly what it was doing. But as it now began to press its rude inquiries upon the Cardinal, the image of an elephant was succeeded in my mind by that of Balzac's orangutan playing a violin. The crudities of the governmental trespass would soon appear more vividly.

For two reasons, Cardinal Krol did not reply to Mr. Hirsch's ultimatum. He did not agree that NLRB had any legal power over church schools. Moreover he was not the employer of the teachers. Under Church law, only the parishes employ them, i.e., the pastors. Pastors of five parishes which operated elementary schools sought legal counsel.[1] Whatever disagreements may have arisen between

---

1   Herbert G. Keene, Jr., an expert in labor relations law; C. Clark Hodgson, Jr.; James E. Gallagher, Jr.; and I undertook this task.

the Association and some parishes, could *government*, the pastors asked, lawfully inject itself into the matter? On January 20, the five pastors went into federal court to seek an injunction, on religious-liberty grounds, to put a stop to NLRB's attempt.

As trial approached, we plainly faced a sticky job in trying to get the pastors free from the toils of the Labor Board. At the outset, indeed, our trial judge, Donald Van Artsdalen, had remarked: "This is a labor case, not a constitutional case." If it was "a labor case," then the parishes were faced with lengthy and costly NLRB administrative proceedings, even though no problems of wages, hours, or conditions of employment were involved but solely the question of whether the Association should be the "bargaining representative" of the teachers. Under NLRB's own rules, constitutional rights, if any, of the pastors, the parishes, and the Church could not be considered in NLRB proceedings. Only "labor law" questions could, and constitutional questions would be heard by a court only after the administrative proceedings. This sort of process is known to lawyers as "exhaustion of remedies." The Supreme Court, long ago taking note of the multiplication (if not metastacizing) of specialized governmental agencies in our society, and considering them to be repositories of expertise in their fields, had laid down the general rule that people complaining of actions of an agency could not come right into court on the matter but would first have to go through proceedings with the agency—i.e., "exhaust" their remedies there.

This "exhaustion of remedies," while it helps reduce burdens on courts, sometimes exhausts the resources of victims of agency actions. In our case it would be not merely extremely burdensome for the pastors to be put to NLRB proceedings; it would also be futile. NLRB had already made up its mind on the key question of whether it had jurisdiction over the church educational ministries. It said it had. Would NLRB jurisdiction over church schools be injurious to religious liberty? That was obviously a constitutional question and therefore a question for a court. Judge Van Artsdalen decided to let trial proceed so that evidence on that question could be presented. Our job now would be to strobelight our case to bring into sharpest visibility that it was a *religious organism* which government was trying to regulate and that the many thrusts of its regulatory scheme would mortally wound that organism. Only then could we hope that the court would act to protect the schools.

To a handful of witnesses—the Archdiocese's top educator, a canon lawyer, and the pastors—fell the task of revealing the organism on which government was seeking to place its regulatory hands. They moved the case to new ground. While the government attorneys portrayed the schools and teachers to the court in secular terms, our witnesses explained to the court what the schools are under the law of the Church. Canon lawyer Father James A. Grant explained the nature of a Catholic parish within a diocese and noted that this organizational structure is "unlike that of any common secular authority." It was essential that the court would understand: "The tradition from which this structure springs is separate from our common law traditions and *must be understood in its own setting and on its own terms.*"

As the Church witnesses began to develop a true picture of the schools, a line of comprehension began to be passed. Monsignor Francis B. Schulte, Archdiocese Superintendent of Schools,[2] approached the nature of the schools from a different angle—that of the actualities of their lives. They would not exist except for their religious mission. Placing in evidence the 1972 Pastoral Letter of the American Bishops, "To Teach As Jesus Did," Schulte described Catholic education as "an expression of the mission entrusted by Jesus to the Church He founded," and the Catholic school as "a single community of faith, in which all employees work commonly for the religious ends for which the schools are established." Religion pervaded the entire curriculum.

These testimonies flatly contradicted NLRB's 1977 pronunciamento on Catholic schools:

> The Board's policy is to decline jurisdiction over religiously sponsored organizations "only when they are completely religious, not just religiously associated." . . . [T]he major part of the elementary school curriculum is devoted to the same kinds of nonreligious subjects as are taught in public schools .

---

2   He is now Archbishop of New Orleans.

. . [T]he subject of religion accounts for less than 15 percent of the schools' weekly schedule. . .[3]

Here again the orangutan was showing itself: NLRB was saying it knew more about the schools than the people who lived the lives of those schools. A governmental body would decide that, apart from a formal religion course, the curriculum and community and discipline of a religious school were really secular. All that, of course, being a *religious* judgment by a body constitutionally required to avoid religious judgments.

On July 7, 1977, Judge Van Artsdalen handed down his decision. NLRB was "permanently enjoined from asserting its jurisdiction over the parish elementary schools of the Archdiocese of Philadelphia." He had come to conclude "without the slightest hesitancy, that the parish elementary schools are profoundly religious in character." Turning to the National Labor Relations Act, he said it was "certainly not intended to regulate religious activity as such; its purpose was to secure industrial peace through compulsory bargaining." Applying it to religious schools would make interference with religious activity "inevitable." NLRB's requirement of segregating the lay employee teachers into a separate bargaining unit "burdens the free exercise of the Church schools' belief in a single undivided community of faith." Further, to "governmentally compel the pastors or the Archdiocese to bargain with a union over ecclesiastical concerns would certainly . . . constitute a restraint upon the free exercise of religion." Van Artsdalen was concerned over compulsion upon the pastors to bargain respecting "terms and conditions of employment"—which could readily involve NLRB in matters of curriculum and teacher discipline—matters "of central concern to the religious mission of the Church." He noted the linkage between salaries and workload, between workload and class size, between class size and range of offerings, between range of offerings and curriculum as well as admissions policies. With *Wisconsin v. Yoder* as precedent, he decided in favor of the pastors.

This decision did not end the case, NLRB appealed to the United

3   227 NLRB No. 177 (1977).

States Court of Appeals for the Third Circuit. Meanwhile NLRB had suffered a like setback from a federal court in its effort to force its jurisdiction on the schools of the Catholic Diocese of Scranton.[4] While our Philadelphia case pended in the Third Circuit, the Supreme Court of the United States handed down a decision in a similar NLRB endeavor involving schools of the Archdiocese of Chicago. By a vote of five to four, the Supreme Court held that teachers in schools operated by a church who teach religious and secular subjects are not within the coverage of the National Labor Relations Act.[5] Since "serious constitutional questions" might arise from such coverage, there would need to be a clear expression that Congress intended the coverage. The Court found no such clear expression. It held schools like the parishes' to be not under the act, hinting, but not holding, that applying the act to them would violate the Constitution. We were happy over the Supreme Court's decision. We were happier still over Judge Van Artsdalen's far stronger opinion.

Today I reflect upon the pastors' suit, the trial and its outcome with a certain excitement. It is to the lasting credit of Cardinal Krol and the five pastors in this case that government jurisdiction over the church's ministry to children was challenged at the outset, instead of abiding (as some dioceses did in parallel cases) the outcome of NLRB proceedings. Madison had warned against compromises where government threatens religious liberty, "[I]t is proper," he said, "to take alarm at the first experiment with our liberties. . . . The free men of America did not wait until usurped power had strengthened itself by exercise, and entangled the question in precedents. *They saw all the consequences in the principle, and they avoided the consequences by denying the principle.*"[6]

The Catholic bishops of Pennsylvania in November 1978, in the aftermath of the Pennsylvania NLRB cases, published a statement

---

4   *McCormick v. Hirsch*, 460 F.Supp. 1337 (M.D.Pa. 1978).

5   *NLRB v. Catholic Bishop of Chicago*, 440 U.S. 490 (1979).

6   James Madison, *A Memorial and Remonstrance Against Religious Assessments*, in D. Davis, *Original Intent*, app. 175–81.

condemning governmental intrusions upon religious ministries and religious life, saying:

> . . . under our American constitutional form of government the Church should not feel that it must live by sufferance but should instead insist that, as it commits itself to live according to the law, so must government. As the Church ought never seek or accept favors by grace of administrators, so it should be forceful in requiring governmental administrators to follow statutes and to observe the Constitution. Those individuals are public servants, and they have no power except that given them by constitutional statutes. . .

It is an unhappy fact that some Catholics in positions of influence attacked that statement as alarmist. Their quip that "Christ came to save us, not to exempt us"[7] disclosed their belief that religious liberty is merely a matter of exemption. The Pennsylvania bishops believed it a matter of right.

Our happiness over the outcome of *Caulfield v. Hirsch*[8] (that was the name of our case) was tempered, however, by thoughts of the hard battle which had had to be fought to get the parish schools free from a statute whose words did not exempt them, a secular act written broadly enough to include them. Judge Van Artsdalen had ruled in their favor on broad constitutional grounds; the Supreme Court had ruled in favor of the Chicago schools on the narrow ground that it doubted that the Congress intended to include religious schools. But legislatures everywhere are daily busy grinding out myriad laws, not a few of which—like the National Labor Relations Act—inadvertently or carelessly impinge on religious institutions or practices. "Well," we reasoned after the *Caulfield* case, "battles like ours, under other laws, may have to be fought again. But where religious liberty is really at stake in those cases, we will have the *Yoder* test to rely on, just as we did in this case. Government will always have to prove a compelling state interest,

---

7   N. C. News Service, November 15, 1978.
8   E.D.Pa. No. 76-279 (Civ., 1977).

even if the law it tries to apply to a religious interest has words which cover that interest."

The basis for our reliance was destroyed in 1990 by the Supreme Court's amazing decision in a case involving peyote.

Retrogression

Hallucinogenic Jurisprudence: The *Smith* Decision

THE PLANT PRODUCED THE BUTTONS which Alfred Smith and Galen Black ate, causing them to be fired from their jobs, this prompting them to seek unemployment compensation, the refusal of which caused them to sue the State of Oregon, whose Supreme Court held they had a right both to eat the buttons and get compensated, which caused the U.S. Supreme Court to say no they didn't, and, in the course of saying that, change the Constitution of the United States for 240 million Americans.

The plant was peyote, or mescal, whose mildly hallucinogenic button-like growths had for centuries been consumed by American Indians (both here and in Latin America) as a sacramental feature of religious ceremonies. Oregon law classified it as a controlled substance the possession of which was forbidden. Smith and Black, employees of a drug rehabilitation organization, participating in a Native American Church ceremony, ingested peyote buttons, and were fired. Contending, in their claim for unemployment compensation, that their button-eating was not misconduct at all but innocent religious observance, their case was eventually heard at Washington and decided by the Supreme Court on April 17, 1990. That the Court ruled against Smith and Black did not occasion great surprise. Sending a shock wave through the country, however, was what the Court did in arriving at that ruling. It scrapped the "compelling state interest" test on which it had based its decision for the Amish in 1972 and handed government powers unheard of in our history to cripple religious freedom. The 1990 decision, *Employment Division v. Smith*,[1] it can now be seen, was the culmination of distinctly secularist stirrings in the Court gradually visible over the eighteen years since the "high water mark" of *Yoder*.

By the vindication of the Amish in 1972, the future of religious liberty in America had seemed better assured than ever before. The *Yoder* decision, dealing with the critical area of religious liberty in education (and repelling the Guardians' aggressions in that area), reached far beyond the question of schooling. The "*Yoder* test" protected religious liberty generally. As we have seen, it said that government must cross a very high hurdle in attempting to place limitations on religious activity—prove that not merely a "public interest" justifies its actions but a *supreme* societal interest ("compelling state interest"). Fifteen years after the *Yoder* decision, the Supreme Court was starting to ignore that hurdle. In 1982 an opinion of Justice John Paul Stevens expressed concern over the fact that the *Yoder* test means that "government always bears a heavy burden of justifying the application of neutral general laws to individual conscientious objectors." "In my opinion," he said, "it is the objector who must shoulder the burden of demonstrating that there is a unique reason for allowing him a special exemption from a valid law of general applicability."[2] Stevens' comment was ominous. He appeared to regard religious liberty as an "exemption" rather than a right. But worse would be the practical effect of his view. Religious claimants are often without large financial resources, or their resources are stewardship funds. Theirs is almost always an uphill fight against governmental agencies with publicly funded batteries of lawyers. Stevens, however, was but one of nine members of the Court, and there seemed no likelihood that his views would win acceptance by any other member of the Court.

In 1986, however, the Court held that the *Yoder* test did not apply

---

1   *Employment Division v. Smith*, 494 U.S. 872 (1990).

2   *United States v. Lee*, 455 U.S. 252, 262 (1982).

in matters of military discipline. One S. Simcha Goldman, an Air Force officer who was an Orthodox Jewish rabbi, had faced court-martial should he observe his religious requirement of wearing a yarmulke indoors while on duty. He sued the Secretary of Defense, claiming that the Air Force regulations forbidding wearing head-gear indoors violated his religious liberty. The Supreme Court, by a vote of five to four, while not denying that Goldman's practice was both religious and sincere, upheld the military regulation because it was a military regulation.[3] The military, said the major-ity, is "a specialized society separate from civilian society." As Nathan Lewin, Goldman's redoubtable attorney, pointed out, the Air Force's position was "a mere *ipse dixit*, with no support from actual experience." Government had not been required to prove its case, prove that it was a compelling state interest which justified the Air Force's action. Justice Stevens' view was now making headway.

In 1988 the Court gave the *Yoder* decision a strange and further limiting meaning. In a case involving the U.S. Forest Service's plan to construct a road and harvest timber on a part of National Forest lands used immemorially by Indians for religious purposes, the Court held that the *Yoder* test applies only in the narrow circum-stance in which government actually tries to *coerce* someone in the practice of religious beliefs.[4] The stifling narrowness of this inter-pretation is thrown into bold relief by the Court's statement that "[e]ven assuming that the government's action here will virtually destroy the Indians' ability to practice their religion, the Constitu-tion simply does not provide a principle that could justify upholding the Indians' legal claims." Here, as in the *Goldman* case, the point to note is not whether the government was right or wrong, but whether the Court made it prove that a compelling state interest justified its actions and that no less drastic means were at its disposal to accomplish what it wanted to do.

---

3   *Goldman v. Weinberger*, 475 U.S. 503 (1986).
4   *Lyng v. Northwest Indians Cemetery Protection Assn.*, 485 U.S. 439 (1988).

In the 1990 peyote case the Court would now go the whole secularizing distance. In many, perhaps most, contests between government and religion, government would now have a preferred position. An opinion by Justice Antonin Scalia, joined by four other members of the Court, held that government need prove no "compelling" interest where its action is "religion-neutral" and "of general applicability." Oregon's drug law was "religion-neutral." It did not refer to the Native American Church, any other church, or name a particular religious practice for restriction. It didn't mention religion or religious beliefs. And it was "of general application." It was a criminal statute which applied to everybody. That was that. Three justices thought differently. They noted that the whole Court had agreed that the use of peyote by Smith and Black was a religious act. They pointed out that the State had not attempted to enforce its drug law against them but had merely denied them unemployment compensation. There was "no evidence that the religious use of peyote had ever harmed anyone." The State, the dissenters reasoned, should have been required to show, in court, what supreme public interest dictated its action.

Scalia, in coming to his startling conclusion, faced a minefield of precedent decisions by the Court, exactly opposite to his ruling. He moved nimbly among the mines, seeking to disarm them one by one. Under his ingenious reasoning, the *Pierce* and *Yoder* cases were no longer religious liberty cases. They were "parental rights" cases, "hybrid" cases onto which religion was merely piggybacked. Having taken the case for the Amish from the trial stage through to the Supreme Court, I had a hard time suppressing the irreverent thought that perhaps the hallucinogenic buttons had made their way beyond Messrs. Smith and Black. If anything got piggybacked in *Yoder* it was the parental interest. The Amish parents resisted Wisconsin in that case not out of some commitment to secular "parental rights." The Amish are not rights activists. The parents were willing to go to jail for one reason only: *their religion.*

Nothing will be served by dragging the reader through the intellectual exercise which constituted the Court's opinion in *Employment Division v. Smith*. Its virtual insouciance in overriding its own prior opinions was really a stunning repudiation of the "judicial conservatism" which the media had attributed especially to

Justice Scalia and Chief Justice Rehnquist. In its departure from constitutionalism, their *Smith* opinion rivaled any prior excesses of "liberal" justices. Apart from its mistreatment of precedent, it thrust the Free Exercise Clause to the back of the constitutional bus.

Casting overboard, then, the vitally important *Yoder* test, the Court's substituted test laid religious freedom open to great danger. To refocus on the new test: *Any* law which is "religion-neutral" and is "of general applicability" will be upheld regardless of how greatly it injures religion. If you will think back now to the NLRB cases, you will see at once the danger. The National Labor Relations Act is exactly such a law—"religion-neutral" (never mentions religion) and "of general applicability" (applies to everybody falling within its terms). But it is precisely in our age, when government is expanding into every area of human existence, that this newly invented *Smith* test is most threatening. The Congress, fifty state legislatures, and thousands of municipalities are constantly grinding out myriad statutes, ordinances and regulations. When, as too often happens, these impinge (intentionally or inadvertently) on religious interests, religion is without defenses unless the laws in question are found to be "religion-neutral" and of "general applicability," or piggy-backed to some other rights.

What about the Guardians in light of the *Smith* decision? They are given a blank check (or sheaves of them). Let us suppose this scenario: A state legislature, lobbied hard by Planned Parenthood, passes a statute aimed at reducing teenage pregnancies and sexual diseases. The statute requires all children to be given information supplied by the Surgeon General of the United States and to be provided with condoms. Religious schools vigorously object on the ground that this requirement attacks basic moral principles prescribed by their religions. The courts, under the *Smith* rule, must require that the statute be enforced. It is by its term religion-neutral, and it applies across the board to all children. But is it justified by a compelling state interest and is it the least restrictive means which government has in order to reduce pregnancies and disease? Answer: Those questions, under the new test, are irrelevant.[5]

As of the date of this book's publication the Supreme Court has had several chances to overrule its *Smith* holding. It has failed to. In 1993, responding to a widespread protest over *Smith*, the Congress enacted the Religious Freedom Restoration Act, and President Clinton signed it into law on November 16 of that year.[6] The Act meets head-on the Court's "religion-neutral" sophistry, noting that "laws 'neutral' toward religion may burden religious exercise as surely as laws intended to interfere with religious exercise." The act's key provision is "to restore the compelling interest test set forth in . . . *Wisconsin v. Yoder*":

> Government may substantially burden a person's exercise of religion only if it demonstrates that application of the burden to the person (1) is in furtherance of a compelling governmental interest; and (2) is the least restrictive means of furthering that compelling governmental interest.

The next case taken up by the Supreme Court where the claim is made that governmental action has violated the right to freely exercise religion may be based on the Religious Freedom Restoration Act. How will the Court react? It is possible that at least some of the justices will say that the separation of powers principle means that Congress has no business telling the courts how they shall deal with constitutional questions. The religious party before a court may run into a particular problem of proving that government's action "substantially" burdens religious exercise. The skepticism which many judges (sons and daughters of a materialist culture) have toward religion may impel them to assume unwarranted roles of judges of religion and rule that the burden on religious exercise was not "substantial." We shall wait.

The "compelling state interest" test is not a perfect guarantor of liberty. It is, in one sense, but a phrase and can be used to justify the worst of governmental actions. Yet its background, both in the *Yoder* and like decisions and in the national debate over the Religious Freedom Restoration Act, sets it off immediately as an interest distinct from the concept of a simply "public interest." So the mere phrase has great significance, and judges forced to employ it as a

---

5   It would be very hazardous for protesting parents to assume that the Court would uphold the parents on a "parental rights" basis.

6   Pub. L. 103-141, Nov. 16, 1993, 107 Stat. 1488.

standard in religious freedom cases should put government upon its proof that what it demands against religion is sustainable only for reasons of the most extreme public necessity (and, of course, is the least drastic means it has for meeting that necessity).

The Power to Destroy: *Ragione di Stato*

CHIEF JUSTICE JOHN MARSHALL, in a Maryland tax case in 1819, said that "the power to tax involves the power to destroy." But his famous phrase reached far beyond an affair in Maryland. It at once recalled the habit of governments from earliest times to mold societies by taxation. It pointed, for all our future, to the same great social potency of taxation. You didn't pick up this book in hopes (or fears) of reading yet another discourse on taxation in the USA today. I am mentioning it only as it relates to our fundamental problem of educational freedom. The molten lead of taxation eddies into two aspects of that freedom. First, our present federal income tax structure is family-discriminatory and, of itself, renders the choice of nonpublic education difficult for many. The greater the taxation imposed on families, the more severe is the burden of that choice. But the federal income tax is only a part of the whole tax burden which families must bear. State income taxes, local taxes of various sorts, property, sales, and other taxes, hidden or indirect, by taxing the family, tax its educational freedom.

Second, the sustaining of governmental enterprises, small and great, is creating a tax hunger which looks to an ever-widening range of subjects for its satisfaction. Public education—or, more correctly, the public school establishment—becomes more costly each year, boosted not only by pressures from unions, but by the growth of expensive perquisites of public school administrators. Hence the constant increase almost everywhere of the school tax.[1] To say that the public school tax on private school parents is "double taxation" is a legally inexact way of expressing a powerful truth. Those parents are bound (a) to pay heavily to support an educational system which they, in conscience (for religious *or* secular reasons, or both), reject and (b) to pay for the education of their children in a form of schooling meeting compulsory attendance law requirements. If they satisfy society's interest in the education of their children through private education, why should they be required to pay for the government schools? Yet, until there is a greater public awareness of the inequity of this, free parental choice will continue to be inhibited by this special tax burden.

To speak of this inequity is not, however, to exhaust the subject of taxation in relation to education. Of equal significance is the character of the tax power as unlimited, and of even greater significance is the character of the tax power as an instrument for molding the citizenry for social ends. This brings us back, inevitably, to the Supreme Court.

The power of government to tax was not deemed unlimited in our constitutional history, but the constitutional limitations on that power came to be more and more disregarded by both the Congress and the Court from 1915 forward. Of particular interest to many parents today is what the Supreme Court has had to say about taxation affecting religious exercise and religious bodies. While, in 1970, the Court had upheld New York's laws exempting church properties from real estate taxes,[2] in 1982, in a case relating to the Social Security tax, it flatly stated: "Because the broad public interest is maintaining a sound tax system is of such a high order, religious belief in conflict with the payment of taxes affords no basis for resisting the tax."[3] Subsequent religious tax decisions coming

---

1   See R. E. Connell, "Challenge to Tax Exemption Growing," *Health Progress*, July–Aug. 1993, 58.

2   *Walz v. Tax Commission*, 397 U.S. 664 (1970).

3   *United States v. Lee, supra*, at 260.

from the Court have expressed an apparently increasing impatience by a majority of the Court where religious tax exemption is concerned.[4] This is all of a piece with what we saw in the peyote case.

"The tax power as an instrument for molding the citizenry for social ends"? We had always accepted the idea that we could discourage evil practices by taxing them so hard as to make them unprofitable. But our tax laws had always wisely lifted their burden from many forms of not-for-profit organizations which serve needs (including religious needs) of people. Increasingly, statists have spoken of such exemptions as "subsidies." Of course, if they are, then the state can exert the same controls over an exempted organization (be it a charity, a school or a church) as it can over any other object on which it expends public funds. The obvious end result of this theory is that the state can control everything in our society. The traditional sensible view of tax exemption has been the opposite. Private organizations, serving good ends and not for profit, should not be taxed. If people organize to do something of mutual interest, without monetary gain, how is that the government's business?[5] In 1983 the Supreme Court moved further not only in repudiation of the traditional view but to create utterly baleful new jurisprudence whose dark portent closely relates to the "pressures" of which I spoke in Part One and to the "American *Kulturkampf*" which I will discuss at the conclusion of this book. The case was *Bob Jones University v. United States*.[6]

Bob Jones, a nonprofit educational institution which participated in no program of state or federal funding, had long observed the belief that God had created separate races and wanted them kept separate as far as marriage was concerned. It carried out this unusual belief by forbidding racial intermarriage of its students and therefore also interracial dating by them. The University did not limit

---

4   See *Hernandez v. Commissioner*, 490 U.S. 680 (1989); *Texas Monthly Inc. v. Bullock*, 489 U.S. 1 (1989).

5   See Dean M. Kelley's excellent study, *Why Churches Should Not Pay Taxes*.

6   *Bob Jones University v. United States*, 461 U.S. 574 (1983).

admissions to whites or otherwise differentiate on account of race. No complaint on account of discrimination had ever been filed against Bob Jones in any state or federal anti-discrimination agency or court. In 1970 the Internal Revenue Service, acting on its own in re-interpreting the Internal Revenue Code, notified the University that since it was, in IRS's eyes, racially discriminatory, its tax-exempt status was revoked. The University sued to contest the revocation. The trial court found the University's religious character to be pervasive, describing the interracial dating and marriage policy as follows:

> A primary fundamentalist conviction of the plaintiff is that the Scriptures forbid interracial dating and marriage. Detailed testimony was presented at trial elucidating the Biblical foundation for these beliefs.

The Court finds that the defendant [the Government] has admitted that plaintiff's [the University's] beliefs against interracial dating and marriage are genuine religious beliefs. Since the Internal Revenue Code exempts institutions whose purpose is religious, the trial court ruled against the IRS and upheld the University's tax exemption. The U.S. Court of Appeals for the Fourth Circuit reversed the trial court, however, and Bob Jones took its case to the Supreme Court.

I won't retell the strange story of the case once the Supreme Court had decided to hear it, beyond mentioning that the government (the Reagan Administration) thereafter told the Court that the IRS had overstepped its powers and had no case at all and that thus the whole matter was moot; that nevertheless the Court, after months of delay in which the national media went wild over the Administration's position, appointed William T. Coleman, an attorney from a Washington megafirm, to argue the case—not *for* any client but simply *against* Bob Jones; and that the Court then decided the case against Bob Jones. The important thing to understand about the case is the reasoning the Court used in order to kill the school's tax exemption.

The Court's decision was not merely portentous; it was exquisitely arcane. In order not to lose you in it, let us instead play a game called "The Bob Jones Decision Made Simple." Let's eight of us sit down and each choose a letter from a list of the first eight letters of the alphabet. I choose to be A, you choose to be B, Justin takes C, Agnes D, Luther E, Ruppert F, Everilda G, and Cuthbert H. Now comes our referee, and he says: "G, please stand up." G (Everilda) does. But the referee says: "No, you're B." He then calls on A, but when I stand up, he says that I, too, am B. So, too, with the other six. What gives? We all protest. But the referee insists that although A, B, C, D, E, F, G, and H are all listed separately, the fellow who made up the list intended A, C, D, E, F, G, and H to be the same thing as B. Now the *Bob Jones* case involved the section of the Internal Revenue Code, the famous Section 501(c)(3), which likewise had a list of eight—these being the eight purposes, at least one of which an organization must have in order to be tax-exempt. It must be, says the list:

A. religious, *or*
B. charitable, *or*
C. scientific, *or*
D. testing for public safety, *or*
E. literary, *or*
F. educational, *or*
G. to foster amateur sports competition, *or*
H. for prevention of cruelty to animals.

Bob Jones University exactly fitted categories A and F. The Supreme Court, like the referee in our game, held all the categories to be B—all of them to be "charitable," even though, on the list, "charitable" was a single category, separated from all the others by the disjunctive "or." The Court (Justice Rehnquist alone dissenting) simply rewrote the statute by erasing "or" and superimposing "charitable" on all the other distinct purposes. The list, and the "ors," were an act of the Congress. But the Supreme Court, feeling the heat of the media firestorm, could not abide leaving it to the Congress to amend its act if indeed the Congress should choose to. The Court, by ruling that all eight categories were "charitable," simply legislated.

What did it mean to say, as the Court did, that all the eight categories (Bob Jones included) are really "charitable" organizations? The Court's answer is the main reason why I have called its decision "baleful." It comes to this: Under the common law, essayed the Court, all "charitable" organizations, to be tax-exempt, must adhere to "federal public policy"; any institution which discriminates on account of race violates "federal public policy" and hence cannot be tax-exempt. Thus the free-wheeling IRS was upheld, and Bob Jones, because of its religiously based practice, stripped of a major means of its support—tax-deductible gifts. But "federal public policy" is a wide-open term, not limited to matters of race. The Age Discrimination in Employment Act states a "federal public policy" against "arbitrary age discrimination in employment"; the Occupational Safety and Health Act, the National Environmental Policy Act, the General Education Provisions Act each express a "federal public policy." If tax exemption is to be denied to a religious ministry on the ground of its violation, not of any statute, nor of the Constitution, but solely of "federal public policy," then all religious ministries are necessarily left to the uncontrolled discretion of IRS to determine what shall or shall not constitute violation of that public policy. Religious bodies, the Court has therefore ruled, must adhere to a *governmental* standard of religious practice, or else be taxed.

The Supreme Court was oblivious, in its decision, to history's testimony that one of the primary tools of religious intolerance which caused our ancestors first to flee England, and then to erect the protective barrier of the First Amendment, was the use of the law to place restrictions or exact penalties on the use of properties for nonconforming religious educational purposes.[7] Justice Lewis F. Powell, Jr., though partly concurring with the majority in the *Bob Jones* case, perceptively noted "the element of conformity" that informed the Court's view, and which to him suggested that "the primary function of a tax-exempt organization is to act on behalf of the government in carrying out governmentally approved policies." He saw tax exemption as "encouraging diverse and, indeed, often sharply conflicting activities and viewpoints" and as "one indispensable means of limiting the influence of governmental orthodoxy in important areas of community life." Here he approached

---

7   See I. H. Hallam, *The Constitutional History of England*, 229.

the epicenter of the Court's ruling known as a danger point by the Founding Fathers, who were familiar, indeed, with the 17th century doctrine of *ragione di stato*, or Reason of State, whereby the prince might violate the common law and rights of citizens for the end of public utility. It was precisely the application of that doctrine to the area of taxation that gave rise to the Petition of Right in England. It was expressed in Nazi Germany as *Gleichshaltung*, or the principle of universal coordination of belief and practice with the polity of the State in all areas of national life.[8] Waiting in the wings following *Bob Jones* are a number of advocacies; for example, the attacking of religiously required sexual differentiation, which attack may likewise offend "federal public policy."

---

8   See C. J. Friedrich, *The Age of the Baroque*, 31. R. Grunberger, *The 12-Year Reich*, 337, 481–501.

American *Kulturkampf*, Uniform Diversity

THIS BOOK HAS WARNED AGAINST Plato's Guardians, made repeated adverse references to "the public school establishment," and spoken of "pressures" threatening religious and intellectual freedom. These highly realistic concerns, however, must not obscure the fact that there are many public school teachers who are people of abundant good will, who love children, and who have high teaching skill. Nor should expressing these concerns obscure the fact that there are public schools in which intellectual quality, good discipline, and a spirit of civility are still to be found. Yet we see an almost universal judgment that public education is now so greatly a failure that we are "a nation at risk."[1] Zealous public education advocates, unable to deny this, propose remedies. All the remedies have a common feature: a vast increase in public funding of a system already gorged in public funds. (Yes, "gorged," when it is realized that *literacy, ability to compute, and acquisition of general knowledge of private school pupils are generally superior to those of public school pupils and are yet achieved at dramatically lower*

---

1   *Report of National Commission on Excellence in Education: A Nation at Risk*, April 1983.

per-pupil cost.) Agreeing that money is the one thing indispensable for public education, the advocates break up into a variety of apostolates, each with its particular solution to the crisis. Some see the answer in restructuring (or re-inventing) education, being sure that, by enlarging the carburetor, realigning the transmission, and adding a valve here, a switch or a cam there, they will have finally got the hang of how to educate kids. Others, like Albert Shanker, see the answer largely in standards, and he points to the high standards set in England, Germany, France, and Japan. He finds the examinations given students in those countries "demanding." While (speaking of biology exams) from 30 to nearly 60 percent of students in those countries take them, and 25 to 36 percent pass them: "[i]n the U.S. only 7 percent of students take the [comparable] AP biology exam, and 4 percent pass." Shanker advocates "emulating the standards to which other industrialized countries hold their students." Yet he perceptively notes:

> But the most important thing that we can learn about these systems is that standards alone are not enough. Students have to be willing to do the hard work necessary to meet the standards. Unless something kids want, like going to college or getting a job, is tied to meeting them—unless there are stakes—the most carefully devised standards will be meaningless.[2]

But while the raising of standards by government may help public education, the truth is that public education is failing intellectually because of its near-monopoly status. It should be regarded as *alternative* education in a competitive market where parents have economically meaningful choice.

But Shanker's words about the "stakes"—about the kids' motivation—bring us inescapably to questions of the kids' values and of how public education relates to their values, i.e., their *moral* outlook. And the starting point in discussing that must be the admission that public education is failing morally because it is

---

2   A. Shanker, "Standards and Stakes," in his "Where We Stand" column, *The New York Times*, May 16, 1994.

Godless. Do not say that I am ranting when I say "Godless." I mean only the simple fact that, with Supreme Court rulings, it *has* to be. That is less a matter of its being forced to ban prayer than it is of having to excise God (and His commandments) as the ultimate reference point for conduct, peaceableness, honesty, respect for others, respect for one's own mind, diligence, discipline. Those of us who experienced the public schools of half a century ago know that it is incontestably true that the mere presence in them of traditional theistic values rendered them morally superior to the schools of today. And that, in turn, yielded an enormous benefit to the nation. The "social decomposition" which William J. Bennett warns may now be overtaking us[3] is due, most of all, to the forced eradication of the inculcation of traditional moral values in the schools attended by the vast majority of our children.

But nature abhors a vacuum and rushes in to fill it. The religious and moral vacuum created by the Supreme Court's 1948 *McCollum* decision pointing to the secularizing the public schools[4] triggered efforts in many states for the providing of religion, in some form or other, in public education. In the *McCollum* case the Supreme Court voided an educational plan whereby ministers, rabbis, and priests could come to public schools and offer thirty minutes of religious instruction per week. The program was financed and regulated by a private interdenominational council, not by the school board. The Court held it, however, to violate the Establishment Clause in a suit brought at the instance of an atheist parent on behalf of her child (who was not, in fact, required to participate in the minimal religious instruction). The Court deemed it irrelevant that the program represented a successfully working consensus in the community, and it utterly ignored the religious interests of the majority of the community's children and their parents. While the Court, four years later, upheld a New York program whereby children were released for religious instruction *off* their public school premises, it held unconstitutional a further program in New York which would have

---

3   W. J. Bennett, *The Index of Leading Cultural Indicators.*

4   *Illinois ex rel. McCollum v. Board of Education*, 333 U.S. 203 (1948).

allowed children to recite, on a voluntary basis, a twenty-four-word nondenominational prayer.[5] Again, the Court was focused completely on the interests ("rights") of objectors and ignored the religious interests of the majority of children and parents.

Engel v. Vitale, the prayer decision, produced widespread cries of protest (characterized by the ever-zealous Professor Freund as "intemperate outbursts"). The Supreme Court in the following year, in the *Schempp* decision we discussed earlier outlawing Bible-reading and the recitation of the Lord's Prayer, attempted an elaborate effort to mollify the widespread sense of outrage over its *Engel* decision. The Court assured the country that it was *not* establishing secular humanism for the public schools; indeed, it said, the Bible could be read for its literary and historic qualities. So, too, comparative religion could be studied, without which "it might well be said that one's education is not complete." The proposition that enforced avoidance of the Bible as the word of God or that "teaching about" religion was religion enough for anyone was palpable ideological (and political) contrivance. The Court's opinion capped all of this by expressing its own *religious* view that, while the place of religion in our society is "an exalted one," that place is in the home, the church, and the inviolable citadel of the individual heart and mind—self and sacristy, in other words, and *not* in the education of most young people.

Efforts on behalf of religious accommodation in the public schools nonetheless persisted, most of these being struck down under the *Lemon v. Kurtzman* Establishment Clause test. Violating the test after *Lemon* have been a Kentucky law requiring posting of the Ten Commandments in public schools (1980),[6] an Alabama statute authorizing a moment of silence for meditation or voluntary prayers (1985),[7] the inclusion of a nonsectarian invocation and

---

5   *Engel v. Vitale*, 370 U.S. 421 (1962).

6   *Stone v. Graham*, 449 U.S. 89 (1980).

7   *Wallace v. Jaffree*, 472 U.S. 38 (1985). Upon remand of this case to the trial court to enforce the Supreme Court's decision, U.S. District Court Judge W. Brevard Hand, in a classic opinion, found secular humanism to be a "religion" and its promotion in the public schools to thus violate

benediction by a rabbi at a public high school graduation.[8] Again the Court in these decisions devoted scarcely a word of thoughtful consideration of the interests of other than the protesters. Justice Scalia, joined by Justices White, Thomas, and the Chief Justice, in the last case, attacked the knuckle-biting apprehensions of the majority that the school's sponsorship of the event would create "indirect and subtle peer pressure" on students. The decision, in the dissenters' view, "lays waste a tradition that is as old as public-school graduations themselves; and that is a component of an even more long-standing American tradition of nonsectarian prayer to God at public celebrations generally."

Thanks chiefly to Evangelicals, some accommodations to religious liberty have been won at the Supreme Court level and in the Congress. The 1984 federal Equal Access Act made it unlawful for public high schools to deny use of school facilities, during noninstructional time, to religious groups if other student groups were permitted such use. A public school district in Omaha denied use of its facilities to a student Christian study club while allowing such use to chess clubs, drama clubs, and many other secular student organizations. The school district said that if the Equal Access Act were applied on behalf of the Christian study clubs, that would violate the Establishment Clause. The Supreme Court upheld the Christian students, and while invoking the *Lemon* test, said it could not be read to bar the students the equal access which they claimed.[9]

Small exceptions such as this aside, the spiritual and moral vacuum in public education largely remains. The strong efforts of Evangelicals to bring about accommodations to religion are as commendable as their prospects of success are speculative. For the foreseeable future, the Supreme Court will continue to read the Constitution as requiring that the life of traditional religion in the

---

the Establishment Clause. *Smith v. Board of Commissioners of Mobile County,* 655 F.Supp. 939 (1987). Judge Hand was (unfortunately) reversed by the 11th Circuit Court of Appeals. (827 F.2d 684 (1987).)

8   *Lee v. Weisman,* 112 S.Ct. 2649 (1992).

9   *Board of Education of Westside Community Schools v. Mergens,* 496 U.S. 226 (1990).

public schools be marginal (e.g., as permitting Bible clubs) at most. In fact, the heavy momentum is in the opposite direction. The vacuum has quite naturally attracted a rush of efforts to respond to the religious and moral needs of children. The kids' hopes, problems, questions, anxieties go on. The public school teachers' hands are judicially tied to nonreligious conformity. The need among public educators for substitute values, once God had been ousted, has led to the adoption of substitute religions.

Values Clarification, Magic Circle, Quest, Skills for Adolescents, and a variety of New Age programs employing Eastern mind-control techniques come to mind. The psychologist Paul C. Vitz has condemned the Values Clarification program for its invasion of familial privacy and the individual privacy of students. He sees it as leading to social anarchy because of its moral relativism. While parental protests have caused many public school districts to abandon or downplay Values Clarification, he warns:

> Unfortunately this moral relativism remains now in the 1990s as part of many programs—especially in health and sex and drug education. The name "Values Clarification" is gone, but the concept under other names continues to undermine the moral life of our children.[10]

These programs are, of course, *religious* substitutes for theistic religion. They seek to embrace all that lies in the domain of theistic religion; the meaning of being (or in some of the programs, being's meaninglessness), how life shall be lived, a world outlook, and secular substitutes for spirituality (e.g., self-awareness). In 1961 the Supreme Court held Secular Humanism (capitalization by the Court) to be a "religion" within the meaning of the Religion Clauses of the First Amendment.[11] That being so, the use of the power, prestige, and public funds of the state to impose it is an even more patent breach of the Constitution than the breaches the Court

---

10   P. C. Vitz, "An American Disaster: Moral Relativity," in *In Search of a National Morality*, (W. B. Ball, ed.), 58.

11   *Torcaso v. Watkins*, 367 U.S. 488 (1961).

chose to find in the minimal religious accommodations in public
school life which it has been striking down since 1948.

Since Vitz wrote his above criticism, a nightmare has moved into
place to complement the materialism and irrationality of the programs of which he spoke. It is the new sex education programs with
their components of explicit information, making available contra-
ceptives, and being bound, in the instruction, to solely materialist
norms.

Efforts by parents protesting secularist programs in the tax-supported schools have frequently met with fierce opposition. In my
own practice I see situations frequently in which parents feel
compelled to protest value-impositions by public schools which
they deem to be immoral or anti-religious. School officials typically
cry "Censorship!" or "Book-burning" when a parent, on moral
grounds, asks that her child not be forced to read a book.[12] But the
public school often deems book-forcing to be its prerogative. In one
case a public high school student was required to read J. D. Salin-
ger's *Catcher in the Rye.* To sophisticated adults the book has had
wide appeal as the sometimes droll, sometimes sad, teenager's
views of life as he finds it. But these observations reflect values not
shared by everyone. In this case, a student's parents did not want
him forced to wade through "God damns" on almost every page,
the use of the name of Jesus Christ as a verbal throw-away, and the
expression of values in respect to sex which the parents thought that
government should not force a child to absorb. His reading of the
book, they said, would be "conduct forbidden by his religion." The
school board, however, contended that the boy must be forced to
read *Catcher* so that his "critical thinking" would be encouraged.
The steadfast stand of the parents (and, likely, the possibility of their
lawsuit) caused the board to back down. It took the actual bringing
of a lawsuit in a similar case to vindicate a student's right against
being forced to read Studs Terkel's book, *Working,* loaded with

---

12   *Mozert v. Hawkins County Public Schools,* 87 F.2d 1088 (6th Cir. 1987),
      cert. denied, 108 S.Ct. 1029 (1988) (frequently caricatured as the "Anne
      Frank, Huckleberry Finn" case).

obscenities. The story of that case has been well told by Nat Hentoff in his recent book, *Free Speech for Me But Not for Thee*.

The growing prevalence of the forceful imposition of secularist values on public school children (truly "mere creatures of the state") brings to mind two points. The first relates to parents. I have spoken here of "parental" rights and of arrogant abuses of these rights by school districts. Yet I must pause to ask *which* parents are those I have in mind. As we raise our swords to lead a crusade for "parents," we had better look back to see who's following us. Indeed, not all parents want the accommodating of religion in the public schools—or anywhere else. We are more and more a materialist, hedonist, and, indeed, mediaized, mindless society. But regardless of whether parents who hold to traditional values are in the majority (I suspect they are), Supreme Court holdings relating to religion in the public schools have so skewed the meaning of the Establishment Clause that, in public education, liberties of mind and religion are to a disturbing extent obliterated. My second point, therefore, is that the Court has caused the Establishment Clause to contradict the Establishment Clause. That is, the Court, in its decisions on religion in the public schools, has ruled that the clause mandates that even the most miniscule incidents of it (posting a copy of the Ten Commandments, a rabbi's graduation invocation, a moment of silence for prayer or meditation) must be antiseptically excised. The Court has also ruled that secular humanism is a religion. But its decisions casting out every vestige of observance of theistic religion necessitate an incoming permeation of public education with the substituted secularism.[13] But that religion, too, is forbidden by the Establishment Clause. It is obvious that if serious regard is yet to be had for the life of spirit and mind of most children, that contradiction must be faced up to, and a corresponding recog-

---

13   The Court's latest pronouncement in a religious liberty case carries its view of "establishment" to the extreme of denying a Hasidic Jewish community accommodation to its religious needs through a statute rendering its incorporated village a public school district. *Board of Education of Kyras Joel Village School District v. Grumet*, 114 S.Ct. 2481 (1994).

nition of the liberating force of the Constitution's clause protecting the free exercise of religion.

It is to be hoped that retrenchment in the Court's Establishment Clause views will not need to be considered in relation to another aspect of governmental overreaching in education, both public and private. This development, not yet fully in place as a matter of our laws, usually goes under the label of "diversity." At the level of institutions of higher learning, "diversity" regulations are now being pushed as obligatory upon colleges and universities, public and private. The "diversity" regulations have been in part the invention of several of the regional college accrediting bodies. These ostensibly private organizations are, in legal fact, quasi-governmental bodies because their power to grant or deny accreditation to an institution is the key to whether the institution, or its students, may participate in federal funding of various kinds. The regional accrediting bodies had never been considered to be regulatory bodies and were held limited in their actions to what had traditionally been deemed academic concerns. In 1990 Westminster Theological Seminary, a major Calvinist institution which, for 36 years, had enjoyed accreditation by Middle States Association of Schools and Colleges, found its accreditation suddenly revoked. Middle States' reason: Westminster had disobeyed Middle States' order to place a woman on its governing board. Westminster's reason for refusal: the tenets of its religion required that its board consist solely of ordained elders, and only males could be ordained elders. Westminster won its fight. The perceptive U.S. Secretary of Education, Lamar Alexander, scotched Middle States' arrogant assumption of power, suspending *its* accreditation with the federal government. That ended that, but within two years a far bolder assault on academic freedom has been seen in the "Statement on Diversity" by the Western Association of Schools and Colleges ("WASC"). This, in the name of cultural "diversity," moves in upon the life and integrity of public and private colleges and universities by requiring rearrangement of student bodies, staffs, faculties, and governing boards—all in order to meet WASC prescriptions on "representativeness"—i.e., institutions must rearrange student bodies, staffs, faculties, and governing boards in order to make them "representative" of all "groups" in "the region." The "groups" are listed as "race, gender, sexual orientation, ethnicity, socioeconomic class, age and religious belief." The regulations also impose *WASC*'s notions of what, in the life of a school, constitutes good conduct, collegiality, proper intellectual and social life. They emphasize "non-Western and non-European values." Venturing into what *WASC* considers educational "quality," the regulations state: "This concern [for "knowledge, evidence and truth"] should not be undermined by *particular judgments of ... religious ... groups.*"

Most interesting about the regulations is the manner of their expression. The mode is not typical regulatory jargon. Rather it speaks in broad and loose terms about desirable features of a school—these features seemingly representing a consensus upon which all enlightened educators must be in agreement. The requirement to comply is stated as "expectations." The vagueness of the language leaves college administrators without any definite measure as to what they should do or not do in order to avoid loss of accreditation. There is thus the built-in compulsion upon conscientious administrators to restrict their conduct to that which is unquestionably safe. Since the regulations are not stated in terms susceptible of objective measurements, people of common intelligence must guess at their meanings and differ as to their applications. WASC inspecting terms are therefore given unbounded discretion in applying the regulations. That is, the WASC Statement on Diversity is a blank check placing total control of institutions (including religious institutions) in *WASC*'s hands.

At the date of this writing this matter is an unresolved, outstanding threat to higher education in WASC's huge region (California, Hawaii, and Guam). Its danger lies not only there but in other regions and in the fact that the "diversity" idea—a matter very different from the generally accepted anti-discrimination laws—is starting to be pressed at the elementary and secondary school level.

Beyond 1994

"WHAT WAS WON THAT DAY on the Normandy beaches was our freedom today." So spoke François Mitterand at the ceremonies commemorating the 50th anniversary of D-Day. "Our freedom today"—freedom for what? we must ask. The grandeur of an era of freedom was beautiful to contemplate on D-Day. Not only had Nazi Germany been vanquished but, recently, the Soviet Union had collapsed. Yet we stand before a blank horizon and must ponder what freedom means and, if we have it, to what use we shall put it.

This book, with its narratives and the warnings they imply, has argued but the narrow issue of parental religious choice in education. At its beginning it said that no area of the life of any nation is of greater importance to its future than that of the education of its young. But even those who agree with its argument stand, too, before the same blank horizon, and it is important that, as we do so, we give thought to what features must fill that horizon if the future is to be good. To posit *goodness* as the desirable quality of mankind's coming life brings us at once to two questions: first, as to what the "good" consists of; second, as to whether "good" is utterly irrelevant and instead we shall proceed, *ad hoc* and *ad hoc*, on the basis of mere utility. To a horrifying extent, the world has proceeded on the latter basis, and you cannot read the histories of World War I and World War II without experiencing the futility of utility—disasters of magnificent scope engineered by cocksure materialists. As we read of developments in the United States today in the area of law alone, we see all too realistically the evisceration of what we once, with some confidence, referred to as the Rule of Law. But when five justices of the Supreme Court—Blackmun, Kennedy, O'Connor, Stevens, and Souter—tell you that there is a "fundamental right" to kill a human being, you know that we can no longer say that we Americans live under the Rule of Law. If life, the most precious of all subjects protected by the Constitution, can be thus dismissed in the case of one set of human beings, it can indeed be in many other cases. If life can be thus regarded, the plug is necessarily pulled on all lesser subjects protected by the Constitution. But in the abortion case you see especially clearly the madness of materialism. Imagine highly educated people, who have enjoyed the fullness of free American life and who pronounce such cruel absurdities as saying that what is killed in abortion is not a being whose sole identity is human or that to "terminate" him or her is not killing him or her—masking the killing in deceitful Aesopian language. Yet such is the spectacle of madness we see when blind utility has power.

So I turn to those who are at least rational and who have some feel for, or perhaps at most a wistful recollection of, "the good" as our traditions conceived "the good." C. S. Lewis, speaking of the "Law of Nature," brings me back to the D-Day celebrations, when he asks: "What was the sense in saying the enemy were in the wrong unless Right is a real thing which the Nazis at bottom knew as well and ought to have practised? If they had no notion of what we mean by right, then . . . we could no more have blamed them for that than for the colour of their hair." He goes on to say (and he might well have described the American utilitarians of the hour): "Think of a country where people were admired for running away in battle, or where a man felt proud of doublecrossing all the people who had been kind to him. You might just as well try to imagine a country where two and two make five."[1]

---

1   C. S. Lewis, *Mere Christianity*, 19. Cf. M. K. Quinlan, "Where We Are Now: The Supreme Court Decisions Ten Years after *Roe v. Wade*." Pub.

Or, he might have added, a country where killing an innocent human being is called a "fundamental right."

We have argued for parental religious choice in education (and therefore also for religious liberty) on the confident assumption that orthodox Catholics, orthodox Evangelicals, and Orthodox Jews bespeak a consensus on "the good" in society. I refer to biblically based principles of personal morality and social justice. Differences among us there are; the consensus is dominant. The consensus sets these "orthodox" off from the crazies, the materialists, the utilitarians, those who (on our Supreme Court, for example) espouse the Machiavellian "reason of state" doctrine. As Hilaire Belloc long ago noted, exciting new arrivals on society's scene are often revivals of things tried before which failed. In the Clinton-Gore era we are all too readily reminded of "the grandiose name of *Kulturkampf*—'battle for civilization'" which Bismarck's Germany pursued. The historian Carlton J. H. Hayes describes it as "the anti-clerical and anti-Catholic campaign which German Liberals fought in the 1870's for the secularization of education, [and] the limitation of ecclesiastical authority," a campaign "essentially sectarian," with a firm belief in "the supreme menace of the Catholic Church to the material and intellectual and national progress of a new age so compelling as to justify the taking of extreme and exceptional measures."[2] We are not yet a Bismarckian police state, but militant materialism is pointing us hard in that direction.

In a recent luminous article,[3] James V. Schall notes the view of the American philosopher, Richard Rorty, that the ideal society is a liberal democratic one "in which absolute values and criteria no longer exist." Solely material satisfaction will be worth pursuing. Majorities will determine not only who shall hold political office and the laws which are made but, under the latter heading, shall decide questions traditionally regarded as moral questions. Schall

No. 17, *AUL Studies in Law and Medicine* (1983).

2   C. J. H. Hayes, *A Generation of Materialism.*

3   J. V. Schall, "The Threat Posed By Modern Democracy," June 1994, *Homiletic & Pastoral Review*, 31.

then turns to a member of the French Academy of Moral and Political Science for comment:

> Ultimately at its root there is also a kind of nihilism which comes from an emptiness of soul; in the national-socialist dictatorship, and in the communist dictatorship, too, there was never a single action which was regarded as evil in itself and always immoral. Whatever served the goals of the movement or of the party was good, however inhuman it might be.

The commentator cited by Schall was Germany's Josef Cardinal Ratzinger. Schall notes Ratzinger's probing of the question of how, for a democratic society, this nihilism can be avoided, with its totalitarian consequences. He points to Ratzinger's citing of Tocqueville and the latter's seeing "alive in America 'a basic moral conviction,' something owed to Protestant Christianity." Schall then stresses Ratzinger's conclusion (precisely the theme so often spoken by John Paul II): "Democracy can work only if individual citizens have grounded principles of right and wrong, ones not decided by majority rule."

This does not mean the creating of a state church or an establishment of religion. In Ratzinger's words: "The Church's nature [is] that she be separate from the State and that her faith be not imposed by the State, but rest on freely defined conviction." This, I believe, provides us what is perhaps the most important feature for our horizon: the recovery of biblical principles as the guide to personal and societal life— achieved only through the religious education of the young.

And the indispensable complement to that is economic freedom of parental choice and the absence of governmental domination in education. The child is not the mere creature of the state.

Cases

Keyishian v. Board of Regents, 384 U.S. 589 (1967)

Lee v. Weisman, 112 S.Ct. 2649 (1992)

Lemon v. Kurtzman, 403 U.S. 602 (1970)

Lyng v. Northwest Indian Cemetery Protection Association, 485 U.S. 439 (1988)

Massachusetts v. Mellon, 264 U.S. 447 (1923)

McCormick v. Hirsch, 460 F.Supp. 1337 (M.D.Pa. 1978)

Meek v. Pittenger, 421 U.S. 349 (1975)

Meyer v. Nebraska, 262 U.S. 390 (1923)

Mozert v. Hawkins County Public Schools, 87 F.2d 1088 (6th Cir. 1987) *cert. den.*, 108 S.Ct. 1029 (1988)

National Labor Relations Board v. Catholic Bishop of Chicago, 440 U.S. 490 (1979)

New Jersey-Philadelphia Presbytery of the Bible Presbyterian Church v. New Jersey State Board of Education, 469 U.S. 1107 (1985)

New Life Baptist Church Academy, et al. v. Town of East Longmeadow, et al., 885 F.2d 940 (1989)

Pierce v. Society of Sisters of the Holy Names of Jesus and Mary, 268 U.S. 510 (1925)

Schade v. Allegheny County Institution District, 386 Pa. 507 (1956)

Smith v. Board of Commissioners of Mobile County, 655 F.Supp. 939 (1987)

Stone v. Graham, 449 U.S. 39 (1980)

Texas Monthly, Inc. v. Bullock, 489 U.S. 1 (1989)

Tilton v. Richardson, 403 U.S. 672 (1971)

Torcaso v. Watkins, 367 U.S. 488 (1961)

United States v. Lee, 455 U.S. 252 (1982)

Wallace v. Jaffree, 472 U.S. 38 (1985)

Walz v. Tax Commission, 397 U.S. 664 (1970)

Wisconsin v. Yoder, 406 U.S. 205 (1972)

Witters v. Washington Department of Services of the Blind, 474 U.S. 481 (1986)

Zobrest v. Catalina Foothills School District, 113 S.Ct. 2462 (1993)